THE TRIAL OF J.J. RAWLINGS

ECHOES OF THE 31ST DECEMBER REVOLUTION

KOJO YANKAH

FOREWORD BY NANA KWASI GYAN-APENTENG

THE TRIAL OF JJ RAWLINGS

Second Edition Published by Habari Afrika Limited, USA.
P.O. Box LG1290, Legon
ISBN 978-9988-2-7617-1

Design by John Hooper
Layout by John Benjamin Yanney

Publishing Consultants: Nana Awere Damoah & Kofi Akpabli
Picture credit: Felix Antonio

Printed by Type Company Limited, Accra

First published 1986 by the Publishing Division of the
Ghana Publishing Corporation, Private Mail Bag, Tema
ISBN 9964 1 0330 1
Printed by Tema Press of the Ghana Publishing Corporation

US Edition Copyright © 1992 by Kojo Yankah
Published by UB & US Communication Systems, 1040-D Settlers
Landing Rd,
Hampton, Virginia 23669
ISBN 1 56411 039 7
Printed by United Brothers Printing & Graphics Unlimited
P.O. Box 5368, Newport News, VA 12305

DEDICATION

This edition is dedicated to
All those who lost their lives and relations during the 15th
May Uprising and 4th June Revolution in 1979 in Ghana
for their Motherland Ghana;
And to all those who believe that the values and lessons
learnt will be valuable in the pursuit of freedom and
justice in Ghana and other parts of Africa.

ACKNOWLEDGEMENTS

As in 1986, when the first edition was published, I acknowledge the invaluable contribution of Flight-Lieutenant Jerry John Rawlings (Rtd) and his wife Nana Konadu Agyeman Rawlings in the interviews granted me towards the compilation of material for this book.

My gratitude to the many serving and now retired military personnel and revolutionary cadres who offered me invaluable personal information, some under conditions of anonymity.

My thanks to the staff of the Graphic Corporation, the Ghana Broadcasting Corporation, the Information Services Department, and the Ghana Armed Forces who assisted in my research efforts.

For this edition, I am thankful to my wife Nana Nyarkoa Yankah for retyping, editing and administrative support.

Accra

KOJO YANKAH
1st March, 2018

TO THE GHANA REVOLUTION

"I do not know of any greater satisfaction
Than honest and efficient service rendered
To the people in the best interest of
ALL THE PEOPLE".

                    Kwame Nkrumah

"We are the living dead.
We have already given up our lives,
We have laid down, for the cause,
All normal warmth, all placid happiness
As obstacles to our commitments,
Not to ourselves,
But to a greater end...
For the cause of Ghana, we are prepared
To sacrifice our lives, our everything".

                    J.J. Rawlings

CONTENTS

INTRODUCTION
TO SECOND EDITION

Since the year 2000 when the 19-year reign of Flight Lieutenant Jerry John Rawlings ended as Head of State of Ghana, I have been inundated with requests to reproduce the original book published in 1986 under the title *The Trial of JJ Rawlings,* sub-titled *Echoes of the 31ˢᵗ December Revolution.*

The requests have been heightened by the total absence of any copies of the book in circulation, giving rise to all sorts of interpretations.

It is 17 years since President JJ Rawlings handed over power to a democratically elected government in Ghana. Adding to his rule of 19 years as Head of State of Ghana, 36 years have passed since the famous 15ᵗʰ May military uprising took place, followed by the 4ᵗʰ June revolution. Various verdicts have been passed since then, some condemnatory, others in praise, but the obvious fact that Ghana's history has gone through various critical and violent phases cannot be erased. For the youth under 36 years, even perhaps in their early forties, the trial of JJ Rawlings that took place in 1979 is still a mystery, even a myth, or better still exaggerated.

In the building of a stable democracy in Ghana, I consider it relevant, like all developed countries have experienced, not to forget where the country has come from. Other countries on the continent of Africa which look up to Ghana for the torch of liberation our forefathers under Osagyefo Kwame Nkrumah lit need to know why and from where Ghana persists in her development efforts.

Not all that happened in 1979 was pleasant. Lives and properties were lost, like in all mutinies and uprisings. In pursuit of justice and freedom in all historical circumstances, suffering, anguish and losses have been recorded.

I am reproducing this book to fill a vacuum that the absence of this script has created for those who seek information to add to their body of knowledge about Ghana's history.

Some names mentioned in this book have remained anonymous or created in respect of their specific request to remain same.

This is a slice of the history of Ghana. Perhaps, through the pages of this book, Flight Lt. JJ Rawlings may be better assessed.

KOJO YANKAH

FOREWORD

The Trial of J. J. Rawlings is a fascinating book about a most fascinating period of Ghana's history, at the centre of which stands the fascinating personality of J.J. Rawlings. This book was a sensation when it was published thirty-two years ago. It was a bestseller in Ghana and a most sought-after book by Ghanaians everywhere as well as people who, for whatever reason, had an interest in Ghana. This is because the book unlocked (or at least tried to unlock) the enigma of Jerry John Rawlings to the extent that it was possible so to do.

Almost a complete generation later, the book is even more relevant today than when it was first published; the story of Jerry Rawlings and the period of the AFRC and early PNDC periods remain only partially told. Indeed, the social and economic dynamics that produced June 4th have also receded into the mists of time, and with them the man at the centre of this tale. Therefore, the story this book tells has acquired a new urgency and becomes a national requirement.

To the youth who were born after the tumultuous period of Jerry's ascendancy, the man is almost a myth. This is a strange phenomenon; Jerry Rawlings is perhaps the most recognizable person in Ghana and yet while we all think we know him, in reality we don't.

The truth is that everyone has an opinion about Rawlings: the good, the bad, the ugly – and some have very strong opinions. Sadly, even among the most informed section of our population, our opinions about Rawlings are based on that same static one-dimensional cartoon character we encounter in the media, often in the form of headlines.

For those of us who lived through the events that form the subject of the book, the Rawlings we know is the Rawlings of June 4th and its aftermath. The younger generation also knows its Rawlings through different lenses in which are refracted different images of Rawlings that do not necessarily connect to the images carried around by the older generation.

This book does not only refresh the memory of those old enough to remember and provide much needed information for the young, it also fills some important gaps in our national narrative. It has come to light recently that some vital information on the early Rawlings era cannot be traced through the media or other archives. However, even those archives need material such as we find in this book to bring the era to life. Now, in the circumstances, material such as this serves as both first-hand and eyewitness sources as well as commentary on other material.

This is very important. The Rawlings era changed the course of Ghana's history. We don't know what would have happened without the chain of events which unfolded with the uprising of May 15, 1979 and the sequence of consequences whose effects are very much alive with us today. Our democracy and politics as well as economic and social relations have been defined by events and activities with Rawlings at the centre. To know and understand that story is important for reconstructing the national story.

The final point about this book is the author, Hon. Kojo Yankah. These days, most people probably know Hon. Yankah as a politician and the founder of a successful university. However, he is an award-winning literary author and a professional communicator as both a journalist and a public relations expert. This book benefits from the application of these disciplines.

Kojo does not tell this story from second hand sources; he was very much involved as a journalist and participant observer during much of the events which he reports in this book. I was privileged to work under Kojo during his editorship of the *Daily Graphic*, which he briefly re-named the *People's Daily Graphic* during the early days of the PNDC.

Re-reading the book brings back memories long repressed, but also reminds me of Kojo Yankah's powers of observation and recall.

This book is a gift to all those who wish to understand a bit more of the Ghana story.

NANA KWASI GYAN-APENTENG
CHAIRMAN, NATIONAL MEDIA COMMISSION
PRESIDENT, GHANA ASSOCIATION OF WRITERS
MARCH 1, 2018

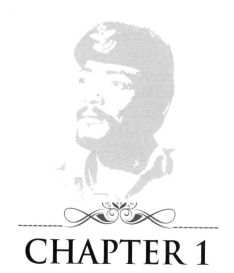

CHAPTER 1

15TH MAY: THE VERDICTS

The time was 5:09 p.m. and the date, 15th May, 1979.

It was a Tuesday afternoon.

A commentator on the British Broadcasting Corporation African Service Programme, **FOCUS ON AFRICA**, was clearly heard saying:

"…How serious this uprising was is far from clear …….. What the motive would be is also less than clear. Ghana is of course scheduled to return to civil rule at the beginning of July, and it could be that some soldiers of the armed forces would like to stop that from happening. It is known that a number of army officers are worried that any future civilian government might vigorously investigate the military for corruption and malpractice during their seven years of administration".

At this time, Flt. Lt. Jerry John Rawlings was behind bars at the Military Intelligence (MI) Annex. He was not terribly disappointed that things had turned out that way. Of course, if the coup had succeeded he would have been more satisfied. Yet anything could happen, he told himself. He would be put on trial, and as long as he got the chance to speak, he knew the whole world would hear his story.

Jerry's wife, Nana, was at home. A couple of visitors, including MI chaps, had come and gone, but at 5:30 p.m. she had to submit herself and their little one-room flat to a thorough search by security agents. She nursed a little baby who was just turning one year, but she endured the meticulous search. Her friends were with her and they consoled her, advising her to move to safer grounds. Her mother was even more worried. Was Nana terribly disturbed by the arrest of Jerry Rawlings?

"Not quite," she said later. "He had been complaining unceasingly about injustices, corruption, abuse of office and other malpractices going on in the military administration".

I looked into her face, expecting further details.

She continued:

"I don't know whether to tell you all this…Look, there came a time when I was hiding my ration of essential commodities from my workplace, Union Trading Company (U. T. C.) from him."

"Why?" I couldn't help reacting.

"You know what he did after work? He would either take an aircraft out diving or spend more time riding horses at the Recce. Otherwise he would just take his dog out into the bush or park somewhere.

"At times, he went swimming or fishing in the Volta River. For him, these activities should have been able to take off his mental attention from the cowardice of man which stared emasculation of the people in the face…

"But," she turned calmly, "the more he got involved in these activities, the more deprivation met him face to face…He told me that anytime he came up-river, swimming, the hungry, lean and dejected looks on the faces of the fishermen wore him down, so what he did was to carry the few so-called essential commodities we had in the house to the people at the riverside anytime he went oyster-fishing. Sometimes there would be nothing at home, so I had to find a way of hiding a few for ourselves".

I was lost for words now. Not even the apparent humour was attractive any longer. Nana rescued me by starting again:

"Do you know that mentally handicapped man who is always parading the street across here?"

I said yes, because you could not miss him. I had recognized him several times standing close to the driveway to the house.

"Jerry insists that we should feed him everyday. He always talks of the way he appreciates the positive and beautiful way in which the man cleaned the environment by picking all the bits and pieces of paper rubbish on the street. So we had to find food for him anytime he came around."

As an after-thought, Nana added: "I should have told you about those fishermen at the riverside. Sometimes, Jerry would even take my needle and thread and leftovers of soap to them." Nana gave a dry smile which was mixed with pity.

To a certain extent, I was beginning to see why May 15 had to come. Nana supplied the right words:

"Personally, I am not surprised at his action. To be honest, I didn't know of his plans but I believed then that diving in the river and riding horses didn't help him much. He may have been looking for a way out of the situation. The wealth and the resources of Ghana matched by the injustices and deprivations shot him in the face…."

"Could one describe it as disillusionment?" I cut in.
"Yes. Probably more than that, thinking that people who got a chance to rule this country cared only about their personal comforts".

In Accra, rumours went wild even long before the official statement was released. The few people who heard the shots around Burma Camp sent the message down.

Some workers found it safe going back home. At the Makola market in the heart of the city, commotion was the order of the day. With rumours that some of the soldiers were marching into town, most traders abandoned their wares in a desperate attempt to seek dear life.

At the Ghana Broadcasting House which was heavily guarded, the workers remained hostages for a number of hours. No entry, no exit.

A release from the Armed Forces Public Relations Directorate had simply said that an Air Force Officer, aided by a handful of airmen, had attempted an uprising early that morning. It went on to say that *"the officer and the airmen had been over-powered and were placed in military custody. In the process, one of the airmen was killed".*

At the drinking bars, interpretations were free. One such had it that General (Mr) Kutu Acheampong's agents had acted to give the 'disgraced' former Head of State the chance to defend himself. Some said it was an invasion from a foreign country which had been repulsed.

The country's nurses had been on strike for a few days in demand for better conditions of service. In the universities, the National Union of Ghana Students was battling with the Government over the shooting of a student by a policeman. Excitement in the nurses' quarters and the university campuses was quite high. Meanwhile, conservancy labourers were laying down their tools: they wanted more pay.

The next morning, 16th May, the dailies carried news of the attempted coup:

UPRISING QUELLED was the banner headline in one paper.

An editorial comment in the ***Daily Graphic*** under the heading, **WHY THIS DISTURBANCE?** said in part:

" *...The shock is deepened further by the fact that yesterday, a three-man delegation, led by Mr. Justice V. C. R. A. C Crabbe Chairman of the Constituent Assembly, was scheduled to present the final draft of the Constitution to the Supreme Military Council at the Castle; a ceremony symbolizing the meticulously planned and the steady steps being taken towards the June 18 election day....*

"*The question then arises: what had the adventurers hoped to achieve at this period when the majority of Ghanaians have all tuned their minds to June 18 and after?*

"*Were they propelled on by mere love of power? Do they have genuine grievances which they hoped can be redressed only through staging a coup? Couldn't they have directed such grievance, if any, through the appropriate channels?"*

The same day, 16th May, the ***Voice of America*** reported the incident for the first time on its French Service at 7:00 in the morning:

"This is the first attempted coup since General Akuffo took office in July last year. Elections are to be held in Ghana next month for a new civilian government."

For some reason the orientation had deepened that the poverty, misery, deprivation and emasculation of the people could disappear with election scheduled for June 18. Everybody seemed to want the military government out. They had mismanaged enough in the past seven years.

It is notable that on May 3rd when the out-going U.S. Ambassador to Ghana, Robert Smith, was saying farewell to Head of State,

General Fred Akuffo, he commended the SMC for "the great statesmanship and skill" it had exhibited "in the preparations towards the handing over of government to civilians".

Mr. Smith also praised the SMC for maintaining Ghana's "fine record on human rights". Yes, a record of oppression, economic rape and exploitation of masses.

As if part of Western Europe was asleep, **Radio France International** chose to keep their listeners in the dark. The 7:00 am news on May 16 simply announced that:

"In Ghana, the people will go to the polls next month to elect a civilian Head of State and a new Parliament. It will be recalled that the present leader, General Akuffo had promised to hand over power to a civilian government with effect from July 1 this year".

Naturally the anxiety to see a civilian government and a parliament mattered more to a number of countries than the degradation to which corruption and malpractice had reduced the ordinary Ghanaian.

On this issue, the **BBC** continued to probe. Its programme, **24 hours** continued with a staffer's point of view:

"There have been moments of discontent among the military, the army, particularly the middle-ranking officers and junior officers, because they fear that the army is going to be investigated vigorously by the future civilian government when it takes office in July. The military administration of the past seven years has become unpopular because of malpractices, stealing, pilfering and corruption...."

The commentator then went to say that since General Akuffo took over power, his government had gone on "*a campaign that laid all the guilt, corruption and malpractice on Acheampong's administration many of whose members are in the present SMC and who made policy decisions with him*".

Radio Switzerland was also concerned about the elections:

"*Government officials in Ghana said the uprising will not affect plans to return the country to civilian rule starting with a general election next month*".

Three clear days later, **Voice of Germany** carried the news of the uprising:

"*Ghana's Army Commander has dismissed an abortive coup early this week as the work of a few misguided people and has called for solidarity in the armed forces…This incident took place just over a month before presidential and parliamentary elections on June 18 which are intended to restore civilian rule after seven years of military government*".

The uprising shook the Ghana Armed Forces. A few of the junior officers and other ranks thought the shake-up was necessary. There were days when in the open Makola market, one soldier told me, women were bold enough to pour urine on a man in uniform who dared ask for prices.

Some officers were quite upset:

"Who must be this joker?" one of them was heard saying. "Does he think he is the only Ghanaian who knows the solutions to what is going on?"

Nana Rawlings heard similar cries on her telephone which kept buzzing:

"Look at what Jerry has done. Who does he think he is?"

Even, very close friends of Flt. Lt. Rawlings expressed similar sentiments when the leader of the attempted coup was named.

Three days after the attempt, the Army Commander, Major General Odartey-Wellington, decorated the officers and men who "quelled the rebellion".

The ***Daily Graphic*** editorial column commented once again:
"The honour conferred on the brave men should revive the time honoured spirit in our soldiers that heroism is always rewarding and that individual precipitate action can lead to disgrace and dishonour".

It continued:
"But for the esprit de corps demonstrated by the remaining units of the Armed Forces, last Tuesday's action could have set the country several decades back from our cherished goal of returning to civil rule and involving all and sundry in saving the nation from economic malaise in which we find ourselves...
"It will be foolhardy on the part of any group to attempt a coup when the SMC has drawn up a programme which leads to the election of a popular government on June 18...

"If the insurrection was meant to overthrow the SMC and extend military rule, we wonder if those involved gave any thought to how civilians whose minds have been tuned up to a return to constitutional rule, would have received a reversal of the situation..."

In detention, Flt. Lt Jerry John Rawlings had no access to any medium of information. No newspaper. No radio. If he did, he would have been more than amused by what a commentator said on the African Service of the BBC on the morning of May 19, 1979:

"According to one report, Flt. Lt. Rawlings wanted the military to stay in power for another two years..."

Months before the planned elections, almost every morning's batch of news included that of prominent clergymen prescribing the kind of leadership Ghana desired. The economic and social degradation of Ghana was well known to all of them, and the least opportunity they got was used for exhortation:

"Rt. Rev. I.S. Lemaire, Anglican Bishop of Accra, has asked Ghanaians to choose future leaders, people who owe a duty to God and their neighbours...
"He said at Tamale at the weekend that only leaders imbued with love for their neighbours could help create a just and happy society...
"Rt. Rev. Lemaire stressed that the country needed dedicated and selfless leaders more than at any other time to help correct its fading image..."

Daily Graphic, *April 11, 1979*

A just and happy society
Dedicated and selfless leaders
The fading image

One wondered why none of the clergymen offered themselves for the position of a leader.

On April 2, 1979, the Rt. Rev. Dominic Andoh, Catholic Bishop of Accra, had advised that aspiring politicians should enlighten Ghanaians more on *"the present economic situation"* of the country, and refrain from making promises which they could not fulfil when voted to power.

"He called on various political leaders to close their ranks and form a united front in order to be able to tackle the country's problems *realistically* in the 3rd Republic…

"The Bishop said that Ghanaians were conversant with the *prevailing circumstances* in the country, adding that it was unwise for aspiring politicians to base their political campaigns on what he called *a pack of lies…*

"Bishop Andoh stated that what the nation needed was *honest, dedicated and God-fearing leaders to steer the affairs of the nation* in the 3rd Republic."

There could not have been any pretence not to know what was going on in Ghana. Yet, the headlines kept coming:

"THE PEOPLE'S VANGUARD WILL ENSURE PUBLIC ACCOUNTABILITY"
"WE WILL IRRIGATE AFRAM PLAINS" – PNP
"PFP TO HONOUR UNKNOWN STUDENTS"
"UNC WILL STOP IMPORTATION OF WHEAT"

Earlier on 6th March, 1979, the ***Daily Graphic*** had commented:
"As a nation, we seem to have reached the lowest water mark in our chequered history. A culmination of events, some of our own making, have thrown our once-promising economy out of gear. Economic mismanagement has no doubt

led to our present economic plight….Our present predicament has also coincided with our preparation to return to civilian rule, the third since independence…"

The soldiers, after 10 years of rule, were going to return to the barracks. The military leaders had their future assured by constitutional guarantees of indemnity.

And the politicians were quite smart with loud promises:

"The leader of the New Nation Party has declared at Ho that when his party is entrusted with power it will establish a junior university in every region…
"In addition, he said a government of the NNP would construct a railway line from Ashaiman through Juapong to Ho, Dzodze and Aflao as a measure to ease transportation difficulties".

Daily Graphic, *6th March, 1979*

Long before May 15, Flt Lt. J. J. Rawlings had been jotting down in pencil some of the thoughts he held. One of such notes suggested that he had a message for May 15:

*"**You will find them everywhere and you ought to know them by now. He may be the departmental head, he may be the Managing Director, he may be the Security officer or the distributor – if you and I will not assume the right to arrest them, let's not expect anyone else to do it for us.***

*"**As I said, each and everyone of us is either part of the problem or a part of the solution…You can neither belong to both nor remain neutral. If you cannot assume the courage to be a man now then forever bury your complaints and remain the slave that you are…***

"We have been deprived of leaders — selfless leaders who think first and foremost of their men, leaders who care first and foremost for the welfare of their subordinates, leaders who feel and understand the plight, the suffering of their people. Instead we have been saddled with nothing but their own pleasures and how to hold on to power and ensure that they retire to LUXURY..."

After his arrest on 15th May, it took some time for Jerry to see a lawyer. The reason is partly because the military government at the time was not decided on the manner of the trial that was suitable. Part of the reason was also that while Jerry's mother was running round looking for counsel, his wife, Nana, was also anxious that a reliable team be hired for whatever trial that was decided upon. However, before Messrs. Adumoa Bossman and Tsatsu Tsikata assembled their points, Jerry himself had begun jotting down his own defence:

"Your Worship, I'm here not to deny my efforts that led to the events of the 14th into the 15th; neither am I here to deny my convictions, my concepts, my beliefs, my conscience. Convictions I share with these honourable men (the other six accused persons), soldiers, but first and foremost citizens of this country...

"Here we are going back to barracks, tainted, very much so, without any dynamic, drastic, radical attempt to purge and punish state criminals who have reduced us to this indignity...

"For me, anything, even death, is better than to be emasculated. Violence would have consumed a lot of lives

and I couldn't bear the thought of one innocent life being lost...

"Your Worship, no change would have been more welcome than now...

"You must know how it means to be an underdog – to be exploited, to be oppressed. The underdog needs protection now more than ever before. Here he is, completely dispossessed of whatever he has, even his humanity. There is, in addition, a feeling of statelessness which has made it possible for aliens and crooks to control state power, the underdog feels helpless ..."

One night, during his detention, Jerry Rawlings received a card from a relative wishing him well. After reading it, he asked for a pencil from one of the security guards and scribbled a few words on the same card. He had two days more to appear before a military court in the Burma Camp and he had to prepare his defence. Part of what he wrote was:

"Your Worship, no matter what you have in store for me and my men, let's do something about the forces; if not, we will end up killing our conscience. A man holding a weapon without conscience can be dangerous...

"Your Worship, if the past and the present can serve as a measure for tomorrow, can you imagine what is in store for us and the coming generation as a result of this inflation brought about by greed and inconsideration?

"The human quality of Ghana will drop. If we had any hopes of making our children any better or as good as we are, they will end up being worse and since the whiteman's culture is here to stay, the cost of maintaining it will rise and rise. I leave it to you to imagine the consequences…"

Months after the hand-over of power to the PNP regime, Jerry had to answer a number of questions from me like:

"Didn't you realize that you missed a great opportunity with 15th May?"

He told me: *"It's not as if one lost an opportunity. The fools didn't know the intensity of the suffering of the underdog. They did not know what was boiling up in people's hearts…*
"They thought they were trying me alone. Little did they know that they were trying the conscience of the armed force, and indeed of the people".

Jerry addressing a crowd from the top of an Information Services Department van

CHAPTER 2

THE RALLYING CALL

"Mr. President, the principal architect and ringleader in the carrying of the mutiny is the first accused, Flight Lieutenant Jerry John Rawlings of the Ghana Air Force Station, Accra. He is a youngman, aged about 31 years."

That was the voice of the Director of Public Prosecutions, Mr. G.E.K. Aikins, at the opening of the trial of which six persons had been charged with conspiracy to cause Mutiny and Mutiny with Violence. A seventh accused was facing the charge of concealment of mutiny.

The date was Monday 28th May, 1979.

The Burma Hall Conference Room of the Ghana Armed Forces was crowded, following a newspaper report that a court martial was opening that morning. There had been quite a level of anxiety not only in government quarters but also in the military and civilian sectors.

Even before the Judge Advocate and Members of the General Court Martial entered the hall, one could sense tension. It was written on the faces of the soldiers who stood impatiently by waiting to hear the message of Jerry John Rawlings.

The civilians were equally anxious. It had never been easy for a set of soldiers to overthrow a military regime. The nearest in Ghana's history was the palace coup about a year before, when Gen Akuffo replaced Gen. Acheampong.

Meanwhile Nana Rawlings had walked in quietly to hide among the crowd.

"I wanted to avoid the television cameras" she told me later. *"In fact not many people knew me as his wife, but some air force officers who knew me made me sit on the second row."*

She had, in the past two weeks, undergone a series of experiences – answering questions from all manner of people, listening to insinuatory remarks, shocked at times by the fact that most close friends of Jerry Rawlings pretended not to know her. Attempts to see Rawlings in his cell were not successful and she had to rely on Lawyer Tsatsu Tsikata for pieces of information about Jerry's health.

In her mind's eye, sitting among the thick crowd, pictures of her husband's sentiments, actions and words raced like a screen play. She narrated to me:

"Far back, when we were friends in Achimota School, he used to complain about people who cheated others. He would not hesitate to go to the defence of

the underdog... He liked sharing. He didn't mind taking off his shorts and giving it to somebody who badly needed one. But in the same vein, he didn't understand why the same beneficiary of this sharing was not prepared to share.... I have known this about him for a long time, and I also know that it cumulated during the third year of Acheampong's regime ..... But then, when he was arrested on the 15th May, his very very close friends who knew him even from Achimota School came asking me silly questions like: has he been giving you large sums of money recently? Does he always stay at home? Have some white men been in the house in the past one week or so?

"If at any one time I wanted to cry, it was because such questions came from Jerry's closest friends who regularly went out with him and who were supposed to know even much better than I did...But I took consolation from the fact that Jerry had always never been a coward. He always told the truth even when at the risk of his life..."

The pressmen were ready. The television and press cameras had been set. All eyes were on the main entrance to the Hall when the court was ordered to rise. There they came Justice Wiredu (Judge Advocate), followed closely by members of the General Court Martial, led by Col. Joseph Enninful. Then came the Director of Public Prosecutions, Mr. G. E. K. Aikins, leading his team made up of his learned friends Mr. Osafo-Sampong (Senior State Attorney), Lt. Col. A. B. Donkor and Capt. T. A. Dartey, both of the Legal Directorate of the Ghana Armed Forces.

The accused persons were marched in, led confidently by Flt. Lt. J. J. Rawlings who was known to quite a number of soldiers present. He wore dark glasses and was holding something that looked like a scroll sheet. Second accused was Leading Aircraftman John Newton Gatsiko; third accused Leading Aircraftsman Sylvanus

Tamakloe; fourth accused Cpt. David Baba; fifth accused lanky Leading Aircraftsman Albert Kwasi Gbafa; sixth accused Leading Aircraftman Daniel Dzibolosu and the seventh accused was Cpl. Ajowiak Ubald.

Particularly for the hundreds of civilians there, Flt. Lt. J.J. Rawlings was a new face. When he was identified as the first accused, the principal architect of the mutiny, curiosity ran high.

Jerry John Rawlings Jnr. was born to Jerry John Rawlings, a Scot, and a Ghanaian mother Madam Victoria Agbotui of Dzelukope, near Keta on June 22, 1947 in Accra.

He completed Achimota School in Accra in 1966 having been an active member of the School's Cadet Corps.

"Way back at the School", he wrote in his first statement after his arrest, "I realized the extent of corruption and injustices in the Nkrumah regime."

When he left school, he changed his mind about flying for Ghana Airways. His mother would not agree to his joining the Ghana Air Force, but he was determined. He left his mother to live with his grandmother. "The callousness and vindictiveness of humanity", he wrote, "stared me in the face".

J. J. Rawlings enlisted as a Flight Cadet at the Takoradi Air Force station on August 25th, 1967. After an orientation course, Jerry entered the Military Academy and Training School at Teshie, near Accra, from September 4th, 1967 until March 18, 1968. He finally completed his cadet training at the Air Force Station at Takoradi on January 25th, 1969, winning the "Speed Bird Trophy" presented to the best cadet in airmanship.

"He kept to himself most of the time while at Takoradi", an Air Force Officer told me. "Anytime I heard him talk, it was about the plight of the poor and the needy – how they could be helped".

Another close friend of Jerry, from Achimota School days, remembered an old joke: "He used to tell his girlfriend, Nana, now his wife, that he did not think she would enjoy being his wife because he was going to be involved in a struggle all his life to help the poor and the needy whom he saw as being unjustifiably exploited. But then, Nana would smile and say "I would struggle with you."

With a short Service Commission in the Armed Forces, Jerry started a full military life as a Pilot Officer – his first rank on Commission. He earned his second rank as Flight Officer in 1971. He earned his third rank (Flight Lieutenant) on April 22nd, 1978 and was attached to the Jet Squadron, Air Force Station, Accra.

"Mr. President", the prosecutor was addressing the Court Marshall, "the first accused had for a long time felt disillusioned about the injustice in our society, more particularly under the Acheampong regime: and so when in July 1978 the SMC was reconstituted with the removal of Mr. Acheampong as Head of State, Jerry John Rawlings thought things were going to be improved. When he realized that there were no improvements in the general conditions of life he was struck with dismay and lamented over what he termed "the tarnished image of the Armed Forces". He regretted that at a time when the Military

Government is due to hand over to a civilian government, the Military Government had done practically nothing to improve the image of the Armed Forces".

The ovation was spontaneous but controlled. The president of the Court Marshall was not sure whether it was safe for proceedings to continue. The general acclaim was that J.J. Rawlings had expressed the true feelings of the junior ranks in the Armed Forces – what he himself called the *conscience of the Armed Forces.*

All eyes, followed by the cameras, were shifted from the prosecutor to the first accused, who sat with legs crossed, serious-looking, but calm.

In his original statement to the investigators, J.J. Rawlings had written that when the then Col. Acheampong stepped in in 1972 to stop the rape of the wealth of the nation he cried "with joy and satisfaction". Acheampong was introducing some "dynamism" into government, "based on honesty and integrity", according to Jerry. But as soon as Col. Acquaye-Nortey, a member of government was spared "for hoarding large quantities of sugar", he began to lose hope. "The abuse of wealth and human dignity began", he wrote.

It was at this point, sometime in 1978, that he began to look for airmen who were expressing similar sentiments about the state of affairs. Discussions continued day and night. Frustration in the armed forces was rising.

"This led him to summon a handful of Air Force personnel including the other accused persons together with Cpl. Daniel Hamidu and Mr. Noi Quaynor and Ali Anum Yemoh, both witnesses in this case, and held secret meetings in a Plantain Grove behind the Air Force Station as to how best to tackle the situation. Evidence will be led to show that secret meetings were held in other places to achieve the same purpose…"

The Director, perspiring under the powerful lights of the television film crew, drew a handkerchief from his pocket and mopped his forehead. He continued, part of the crowd getting restless:

"During one of their meetings in the Plantain Grove, the first accused discussed with the other accused persons his plan to bomb industrial buildings owned by Syrians and Lebanese, cause confusion in the country whereby soldiers and civilians would be expected to join and embark upon looting, and then compel the SMC and senior officers in the Armed Forces to institute committees of enquiry headed by junior officers of the Ghana Armed Forces with a view of investigating the past activities of those Syrian and Lebanese who have deeply eaten into the economy of this country before the hand-over to a civilian government…"

The murmurs of approval were growing louder among the crowd and it was clear that Jerry was winning great sympathy. He listened, unmoved, nodding his head once in a while.

The question of foreign domination of the economy was well-known; and even on the university campuses it was a popular point of concern. The military governments of the time accommodated this situation quite well because of their connivance with corrupt Lebanese and Syrians.

For a few minutes, the Court room became silent as the Director of Public Prosecution read the details of the operation:

"Mr. President, the Prosecution will lead evidence to show that after closing from duty in the afternoon of 14th May, 1979, the first accused person, Flight Lieutenant Jerry John Rawlings picked an ex-airman Mr. Nii Noi Quaynor in his car and drove to the Recce stable where Rawlings signed for a hammer and a pair of pincers. From there he drove through the station to find out who the duty crew were and whether the published officer was the one on duty. On arrival he realized that the duty officer was rather Flight Lieutenant Atiemo and not W. O. Sackey as published. From there he went to the Mess to find out from the Adjutant if Flight Lieutenant Atiemo was on duty as a punishment and this was confirmed.

"Flight Lieutenant Jerry John Rawlings then drove his car home and gave Mr. Quaynor some lunch, then packed his overall, boots, pistol and tools into a kit bag. He left with Mr. Quaynor to the latter's house where Mr. Quaynor also collected his overall and took some money with him. They then went through the bush and arrived at the plantain grove at about 8 p.m. He apologized to his colleagues who had assembled there, namely Gatsiko, Sylvanus, Nick, Daniel, Gbafa, for arriving later than the scheduled time, and briefed them about the form the operation was going to take, i.e. assuming control over the station after arming themselves, taking over armoured vehicles and them proceeding to Recce

Headquarters where the rest of the armoured cars were stationed. He then asked Gatsiko to follow him through the bush to the Air Force Station Ammunition dump where Rawlings broke the padlocks, went inside and collected a box of 9 ammunition rounds and a tin of 7.62 rounds of ammunition. At this stage Albert Kwasi Gbafa, the 5th accused person joined them. Rawlings then shut the door and returned to their rendezvous. Thereafter Rawlings sent for Cpl. David Baba, the 4th accused, with the information that the other person on duty was wide awake, and so Rawlings suggested that they should wait until he fell asleep.

"It was then 10:30 p.m. Rawlings and his group waited until 2:00 a.m. when Cpl Hamidu collected the keys to the Armoury from the sleeping guard and brought them to Rawlings. Rawlings asked Gbafa, the 5th accused person, to accompany him to the Armoury where they opened the doors and collected about 10 G.3 rifles, 10 S.M.G.s (Submachine Guns) and magazines, and returned to their hideout in the bush. The First accused then shared the weapons and ammunition among his men, went and took over the duty station by arresting the duty officer Flight Lieutenant Atiemo and the duty crew men. He was accompanied by the third accused, Leading Aircraftman Sylvanus Tamakloe.

The first accused ordered the duty officer to telephone for the duty vehicle, and on arrival of the vehicle Rawlings ordered the driver to get down, and asked the 6th accused, Daniel Dzibolosu to take control of the wheel. Rawlings ordered the Duty Officer into the front seat and he jumped into the back seat with Gatsiko, Nick and Quaynor.

"They started moving towards the Recce stable. On the way through the gate, Rawlings dropped Noi Quaynor and another airman to take over the gate guards, and took along with him the gate commander. From there Rawlings went with his men to the Recce stable where he arrested three soldiers who were said to be sleeping. He instructed one of them to telephone the Duty Officer, by name W. O. II Asare, and inform him to come to the aid of a woman who was being molested and was bleeding. By this ruse he was able to robe in Asare, and with him they all drove to Air Force Station. There Rawlings dropped the three men he had taken from the Recce, and proceeded with W. O. II Asare to the V.I.P. Lounge of the Airport, where he instructed Asare to order the drivers of the Armoured car to fall in. As W. O. II Asare appeared hesitant, the first accused took over, and ordered the men to charge the armoured cars, i.e. to fill the guns mounted on the vehicles with ammunition. The drivers said the armoured cars were already charged.

"At this time it was getting to daybreak. The first accused ordered the drivers into their seats and the gunners into theirs, while Newton Gatsiko, and the 2nd accused, and another airman took over one of the armoured cars, and Cpl David Baba, the fourth accused and Rawlings mounted the other together with the Duty Officer. From there they drove to the Air Force Station where Rawlings collected the rest of the Recce soldiers and proceeded to Recce Headquarters. They parked in front of the gate leading to the armoured cars garage, near the Square.

At this time, the courtroom was dead silent.

The Director looked up for a second, and continued:

"Rawlings sent one of the Recce soldiers to blow the alarm of the Unit, but when he was told that it was not serviceable, Rawlings sent Gatsiko in his armoured vehicle to the Air Force Station to blow the alarm there, and bring the siren down with him, which Gatsiko did. Gatsiko returned and informed Rawlings that while coming out of the Air Force station he Gatsiko had ordered the arrest of Group Capt. Pumpuni, and Wing Commander Ametepe and Squadron Leader Dedey."

In an interview later, Gatsiko explained that whilst coming out of the Air Force Station at the main gate the guards had been confronted with their hands raised. Upon his enquiry about what was going on, the guards told him that they had arrested those three officers. He then told them to send the officers to the Guard Room.

According to the Director of Prosecutions:

"Rawlings then instructed one of the soldiers to blow the siren, and in the process of the siren being blown the Recce Regiment Commanding Officer, Major Abubaka Suleimana arrived in his car. He was confronted by the first accused and his men. When Major Suleimana queried the driver of one of the Armoured cars as why he was not wearing his beret while driving the MOWAG, the first accused shouted "You are not in command here, I am! You are under arrest!"

"Major Suleimana sensed there was something wrong, got out of his car, and was chased by the MOWAG until he reached the junction to his house. The Major shouted at the driver of the MOWAG to drive the vehicle back to the Square, but the first accused retorted saying "Sir, I am serious, and if you don't stop I will fire at you'. Major Suleimana did not stop, and the first accused fired the S.M.G. (submachine gun) which he was holding.

"Mr. President, evidence will be led to show that Major Suleimana rushed to the Recce Magazine where soldiers were armed with guns and ammunition, and supplied them with armoured cars to quell the operation. Among the officers who were arrested and later given seats in readiness for a dialogue with Rawlings are: Col. Ofosu-Appiah, Col. Coker-Appiah (rtd), Group Capt. Clottey, Wing Commander Ametepe, Squadron Leader Jones Mensah, Squadron Leader Azaria, Lt.-Col. Twum Ampofo and Capt. Owoo."

Murmurs were heard in the courtroom. The Director continued when the noise died down:

"During the course of negotiations, Major Okyere asked the first accused to outline his aims and objectives for the exercise that morning but the first accused replied that it *sounded rather foolish for one to ask him of his aims when people were dying of starvation in the teeth of a few, well fed, who even had the chance of growing fatter,* when the economy of this country was dominated by foreigners, especially Arabs and Lebanese, whom successive governments had failed to question about their nefarious activities. The first accused started talking about wide-spread corruption in high places, and stated that this nasty state of affairs could be remedied only by *going the Ethiopian way"*.

The crowd could not help but cheer. It got so loud that the President of the Court warned that he would not hesitate to stop proceedings.

When the cheers died down, the D.P.P. continued:

"During the course of the dialogue Rawlings used some of the officers arrested as hostages. After a while three MOWAGS arrived through the main gate and surrounded the officer group. There was shooting, and in the process an airman died while another got wounded. Major Suleimana later arrived at the scene and succeeded in getting Rawlings disarm his men. Rawlings put down his gun and was eventually arrested. A draft speech which is suspected was intended to be read by the first accused during the exercise, was collected from his person when he was searched. Details of his speech will be made known during the trial."

The D.P.P. paused, took a deep breath and continued:

"Mr. President, My Lord Judge Advocate, Members of the General Court Martial, briefly these are the facts upon which these accused persons have been arraigned before you .... This state of affairs threw the whole of Accra into *pandemonium during which a number of civilian population ran helter-skelter and some fat Makola women succeeded in out-running the thin ones.*"

The crowd greeted the conclusion of the Prosecutor's statement with laughter – a timely release of the tension which was already building up. The team for J. J. Rawlings was led by Mr. Adumoah-Bossman, but the rest of the accused had not been lucky. However, Mr. Adumoah-Bossman pledged that the Bar Association would endeavour to find counsel for the rest.

On resumption, the accused marched back to their seats after consultation with defence counsel. Jerry was heard barking to the rest to **"straighten up and march like soldiers"**. Despite the anxiety of the crowd, the six other accused persons didn't have much hope. Some seemed like blaming Jerry Rawlings for all this. Adjournment was granted for the court to resume in two days. Various commentaries and interpretations were murmured by the crowd as they left the court room.

History did not allow the full text of Jerry's draft speech mentioned by the Prosecutor ever to be read. But in his own handwriting, as obtained from my research, he said:

"Fellow Citizens of Ghana,
"Now! You listen to me well and good because I am not here to make a speech and I am not here to waste my time talking. First and foremost let me inform you that I am not here to impose myself on 10 million citizens of this country. But I am telling you that I am here today in the history of this country to address myself to military senior officers, all those politicians, all those businessmen and foreign criminals who have used our blood, sweat and tears-the toils of our laboring-to enrich themselves, to drown in wine and women, while you and I, while the majority of us, are daily struggling for survival, yes!

"I know what if feels like going to bed with a headache for want of food in the stomach.

"Let me give you, the struggling and suffering masses, just one little warning. Should anyone or group of you dare collaborate or help exploiting pigs to run away, this country will once more bleed than we anticipate.

"I am not an expert in Economics and I am not an expert in Law but I am an expert in working on an empty stomach while wondering when and where the next meal will come from.

"I am going to prove to you today that it is no longer a question of the military against the civilians, it is no longer a question of the Akan against the Ewe, the Ga against the Northerner. But a question of THOSE WHO HAVE against those who HAVE NOT- A question of the vast majority of hungry people against a very tiny minority of greedy, inhuman, selfish senior officers, politicians, businessmen and their bank managers and a bunch of cowardly Lebanese who will not stay in their country to fight for a cause. But who is a fool? You and I.

"You and I are the bigger fools for allowing such a blatant abuse of human dignity for so long. 22 years after independence, you and I are still hitting our heads on the ground and leaving it all to God to save us one day. Where on this earth had God come to the salvation of a people without the suffering, starving, hungry people taking the law into their own hands!

"**America has seen her brand of a revolution, France has seen her brand of a revolution. Britain has seen her brand of revolution. Russia, China, Iran, all of them. Only the black man in the black African Continent goes on leading his fellow blackmen like a herd of cattle while suppressing them like slaves. Let me tell you today that God will not help you, and the big man will not help you because his stomach is full, his children's stomachs are full and there is enough for them to go and come as they like.**

"Only you can help yourselves."

On Wednesday, 30th May, the Court Martial resumed. There was something very significant this time. On the walls of the Burma Camp, leading to the Burma Hall, posters were conspicuous and early arrivals could not miss the messages. Some were written in chalk:

"STOP THE TRIAL OR ELSE…"
"IF YOU WANT TO DIE, CONTINUE THIS TRIAL"
"REVOLUTION OR DEATH"
"THE STRUGGLE WILL CONTINUE"

But in no time, the military authorities tore all of them down, just in time for the Court to sit. The front-page banner headlines in the daily newspapers spoke of Jerry Rawlings fighting against injustices. The statement of the Director of Public Prosecutions was given wide coverage, much to the annoyance of some members of government. That explained the huge uncontrollable crowd that milled in the hall this time.

They cheered openly despite warnings by the Court President, Col. J. Enninful.

The first witness, Flt. Lt. J. B. Atiemo, confirmed that the first accused had declared that he was prepared to die on behalf of the rest of the accused. The applause grew wilder.

The next morning, the banner headline of the Daily Graphic read: **"LEAVE MY MEN ALONE!…I'm Responsible For Everything."**

The fire caught on. "Here was a real leader", one Corporal Adjei told me later. "In the military, the junior ranks don't like officers who are cowards…Moreover, he was saying something all of us had wanted to say long ago. We only needed a leader and we all identified him in Flt. Lt. Rawlings. Even those who did not know him before came to love him."

The third sitting of the court was on Thursday 31st May. The defence counsel cross-examined the first prosecution witness amidst shouting and clapping in support of the stand taken by Flt. Lt. Rawlings.

Before the President adjourned till Monday 4th June to enable the Attorney-General's Department to find counsel for the other accused persons, he gave what he called a final warning to the public gallery "to desist from any further shouting and clapping." He added that he would not hesitate "to stop the public from listening to the rest of proceedings."

The die was cast. As the accused persons were being marched away, some of the members of the public waved at them, some with fists raised.

Flt. Lt. Rawlings escorts Gen. F. W. K. Akuffo to inspect a guard of honour just before the SMC Chairman flew to Togo (four days before 15th May, 1979).

The seven accused persons waiting for proceedings to start

CHAPTER 3

COME JUNE 4

It was with great difficulty getting two of the seven soldiers who were assigned to guard J. J. Rawlings from 15ᵗʰ May to talk to me. It was not so much out of love for anonymity as the fact that they are "still in the process." I promised to guard their identity.

One of them, K. O. had this to say:

"After Flt. Lt. Rawlings had been arrested for the 15ᵗʰ May mutiny we were selected to escort him to the Special Branch annex where he was locked up.

"While we were with him till 4ᵗʰ June, we very much associated with him and we usually carried messages to and from the barracks. On the night of 3ʳᵈ June, two corporals came to inform me that I had to be ready to help release Jerry on the 4ᵗʰ. I consented."

The other, C. F. said: "My section Commander briefed us that we had to be very vigilant on Flt. Lt. Rawlings, so we put him under close arrest…Soon, because I was the only smoker, it became much easier communicating with him…We shared cigarettes and later used the opportunity to discuss details of his motives with us…We got very interested and we grew to like him. One night, two soldiers came to inform us that something was going to happen and they would need our co-operation. I was in agreement."

Exactly at 2:30 a.m. on June 4, the Special Branch man in charge of the key to Jerry's cell alarmed the guards that soldiers were shooting themselves in the Burma Camp and that Jerry should not be made to know. But the boys were on their guard.

An hour and half later one of the guards heard a familiar voice. It was one Lieutenant and three other ranks who had arrived. The man holding the key to Jerry's cell had disappeared. So K.O. and another sergeant found an iron bar with which they hit the lock until it opened. Earlier, one of those who arrived wanted to fire into the lock but Jerry stopped him.

"When the door was opened, Flt. Lt. J.J. Rawlings was 'dragged out.'

"We took him straight to Broadcasting House, 500 yards away where our men had stationed," K. O. said.

Flt. Lt. J.J. Rawlings had been jotting down notes, but what he read to wake up Ghanaians to his call was disjointed, disorganized and mostly extemporaneous. He was excited and anxious and panting.

According to one Sergeant, "We just wanted him to say something to Ghanaians, that something was going on. He was already popular with the trial so he became our national leader."

Asked who led the group to move on June 4, the Sergeant simply said:

"It was a popular uprising."

The plot to strike must have been hatched soon after 15th May, during the burial of the only airforce man who died, LAC Osei-Tutu. In the midst of tight security, whispers went round that if Jerry had informed a lot of people, May 15th would have succeeded. Despite the fact that all those involved in the whispers were rounded up and locked in cells, the message went down. So that, with the tension raised by the proceedings at the trial, the first shot in Burma Camp was enough indication that the revolutionary forces were on the move.

The first announcement of Jerry John Rawlings which fired the consciences of several other soldiers and civilian masses went like this:

"The ranks have just taken over the destiny of this country. Fellow officers, if we are to avoid any bloodshed, I plead with you not to attempt to stand in their way because they are full of malice, hatred hatred we have forced into them through all these years of suppression. They are ready to get it out, the venom that we have created. So for heaven's sake do not stand in their way. They are not fools. If you have any reason to fear them, you may run. If you have no reason to feel guilty, do not move. Like I said, they are not fools. The judgement will come….This is what will take place in every unit outside Accra. All units are to choose their own representatives to the new Revolutionary Council that has come to replace the Supreme Military Council which is no more…"

Rawlings did not forget that electioneering campaigns were still going on:

"The Ghana Armed Forces will be handing over to the civilians in due time. Elections will still take place…But before the elections go on, justice which has been denied to the Ghanaian worker will have to take place, I promise you. **You are either a part of the problem or a part of the solution. There is no middle way…**"

Nana Konadu Agyeman Rawlings had virtually no other option than to move out of their house. She was with a baby a year old, her mother and friends were naturally worried. They succeeded in prevailing upon her to take refuge. No longer had she left than three officers drove into the house apparently to take her hostage until "Jerry stopped his nonsense".

But Jerry didn't stop his "nonsense." It was a popular uprising whose flame he had fired. The ranks had taken over, he had said. This was the first time in the history of the country that the ranks had given expression to their disgust with the rot in the Ghana Armed Forces and the society at large.

It was the ranks who decided that Flt. Lt. J. J. Rawlings should be the undisputed leader of the new Revolutionary Council that was to rule the country.

Opposition there naturally was. The Army Commander, Major-General Odartey-Wellington, could not have taken it lying low. He mobilized opposing forces, drove into Broadcasting House just over an hour later and announced that the coup had been foiled:

"I would like to add that all officers and men, whether they were actively involved in the uprising or not, are to report back to their units whilst steps are being taken to iron out any grievances or any alleged injustices."

Did the Army Commander know or did not know that at the trial of J. J. Rawlings the chief prosecutor had mentioned injustices? And that the soldiers had cheered?

About half an hour later, Major-General Odartey-Wellington was back in the studio with an appeal to all members of the Ghana Armed Forces to stop firing.

"I also urge Flt. Lt. J. J. Rawlings and any following he has with him to meet me at headquarters."

Rawlings and his men would have been fools to honour this invitation. The fighting continued and the Army Commander himself was chased to the Nima Police Station where he was shot dead.

Later in the afternoon, an unidentified voice told the Nation on radio that the revolutionary forces were still in power and that all former SMC members and leading functionaries should report to the Police "for their own safety."

It was the Chief of Defence Staff, Major-General Hamidu who cleared the doubts once and for all:

"I am happy to announce that the hypocrisy of the Acheampong and Akuffo regimes…has been brought to an end. All members of the said regime are to report to the Air Force Station or the nearest Police Station now for their own safety. We wish to assure you that elections will go on as planned…It is in the national interest, therefore, that we are pursuing this course. We have suffered for far too long…May God bless this Nation."

The next morning, the **Daily Graphic** wrote in its editorial column:

"Ghanaian woke up to what certainly has all the features of a peoples' revolution…

"For far too long the poor who form the majority have lived on the verge of starvation. It has been virtually impossible for most people to eat, care for the sick and clothe themselves within their income because of high cost of living…

"The market women, shop owners, and a host of traders that emerged in recent times just could not care about the suffering of fellow Ghanaians. There was no hope in sight for the poor. No one heeded his cry for mercy and justice…*It is rightly believed that men in high positions are party to this exploitation of the masses.*

"Morals and discipline had virtually broken down and the Ghanaian had lost his sense of propriety honesty and good-naturedness.

"With all these, what happened yesterday was not unexpected by the broad masses of the people who had been crying for justice".

Were the masses expecting a change? If, as the *Graphic* says, they were expecting a saviour, then it means it was only the rich, upper middle classes who were very anxious to take over state power through the elections. The masses had been left leaderless. It was certainly not an accident that the *Daily Graphic* found itself coming face to face with the truth – that the masses would welcome the Revolution. The trial in Burma Camp had lit the fire for the People's Revolution, and the *Graphic*, no matter the editor's ideological position, could not have denied the truth.

Meanwhile, the foreign media called the intervention as an act of rebels. They carried various curious headlines and leads:

Hindustan Times, India, wrote:
"Ghana Rebels in Firm Control"
"A group of rebel officers who launched a coup in Ghana yesterday said today they were in firm control and had set up a new Revolutionary Council".

6th June, 1979
Indian Express, 6th June, said:

Junta Stages Coup in Ghana, poll on June 18
"Rebel troops who staged a coup in Ghana last night said today that elections planned for June 18 to return the country to civilian rule should go on as scheduled".

The Statesman (New Delhi) carried an Associated Press (AP) report from London which said:

'The Commander of Ghana's Armed Forces was killed and the Head of State stabbed in the coup that brought Flt. Lt. Jerry John Rawlings and his followers to power on Monday".

The Indian Express, also quoting Associated Press, used the curious headline:

"Leftists in Control in Ghana"

.... and said in part of the story:

"Rawlings was jailed in mid-May after his first attempt to seize power. Little is known about him but there is speculation here that the coup will bring Ghana under left-wing control".

This is manipulation of news alright. And the Associated Press of America must have had its own reasons spreading this kind of "speculation".

Yet, even more intriguing was a ***Reuters*** (London) report published in the ***Times of India*** of June 8:

"First travellers...reported only a few casualties in the barracks coup that brought a crusading radical, Flt. Lt. J.J. Rawlings to power at the head of a revolutionary council of low-ranking soldiers...

"The travelers report that Flt. Lt. Rawlings appeared on television accompanied by gun-toting guards to announce his aim of cleaning up Ghana, which is beset with economic problems and corruption...

"The youthful Flight Lieutenant was described by several people as a mystery figure. Some said he was half-Scottish, half-Ghanaian; others believed he was the son of a German father and Ghanaian mother."

In the American press, the events in Ghana received quite an attention.

The **New York Times** carried a story from a correspondent in Ndjamena Chad, part of which read:

"Flt. Lt. Rawlings is described by friends and associates as an idealistic, bitter young air force officer, disillusioned by the corruption of his superiors and the way they have tarnished the image of the once proud Armed Forces during their seven years of rule."

The headline of the 6th June, **Washington Post** read:
"Officer Claims Leadership in Ghana"

Clearly showing a distance or a slant from the realities in Ghana, the paper, whose correspondent lived in Abidjan, said:

"A junior Air Force Officer proclaimed himself Chairman of Ghana's new revolutionary council today and warned in a broadcast over Ghanaian radio that anyone threatening the Council 'will be shot'…

"Rawlings' takeover marks the second overthrow of a military government by disgruntled junior officers in the bankrupt West African country in less than a year."

The paper didn't say which was the first one in the year; but at least admitted that Ghana was bankrupt.

On its side, the *Washing Star* attributed the coup to the work of "rebel Air Force Officers."

And to create the usual "necessary" atmosphere for the new regime to be attacked, the respectable *New York Times* quoted the American UPI (United Press International) news agency as saying that the reporter who fled Ghana just before the border was closed said today that hundreds of lives were lost in Monday's coup."

One interesting bit about content analysis is the diversity of reportage one comes across.

It is under a close examination of these various reports that one realizes that communication must be nothing else but purposive.
Reaction to the June 4 attack on the corrupt system which was operating was also mixed in the British press.

On the *BBC,* the discussion admitted wide-spread corruption in the Ghana Armed Forces and asked the question:

"Is Flt. Lt. Rawlings the luckiest man in the world or is he the match that ignited the flame of resentment for the system of military rule which Ghanaians have experienced of over the past seven years?"

Yet the *Scotsman,* on 7th June, published:
"The country (Ghana) seems to have lost its way. Why should

human blood be wasted when the country's new leaders apparently planned to do exactly the same as General Akuffo and allow election to take place? The whole coup seems to be a complete waste of time."

The ***Nigerian Tribune*** (11th June):
"The coup is bad for Ghana, bad for Africa and an unpardonable blunder at this point in time…The well-laid out political programme in Ghana might be disrupted by the new development…

"Ghanaians should not allow themselves to be misguided by power-drunk fellows to seek another chance to further plunder Ghana… Ghana, indeed Africa, requires more serious planning and dedication from seasoned leaders to take her out of the woods to which sporadic military interventions have sentenced her."

The Daily Times of Nigeria, wrote:
"…The Coup is an exercise in futility, unpatriotic, unnecessary, and a calculated measure to frustrate the transitional process…What valid reasons could the new government put up for ousting General Akuffo's administration…It was ill-timed, unfortunate and unwarranted and designed to complicate the already unstable situation in Ghana."

No matter what the foreign press said, the Ghanaian masses had reason to support the action of June 4. When the ***BBC African Service*** read the editorial of the ***Scotsman*** on its programmes, it was bombarded with wild reactions from Ghanaians who lived and suffered in the country.

One such reaction, sent by Andrew Quist, was read on **FOCUS ON AFRICA** on 13th June:

"I must protest strongly against such uninformed and stupid view about the coup in Ghana. If whoever wrote the editorial had bothered to do a little research before making such unreasonable pronouncements he would have answered his own questions about the reasons for the coup. It was not a coup for a coup's sake. What insulting rubbish!

"General Akuffo and all Ghanaians are well aware of Flt. Lt. Rawlings and his main reasons for staging the coup. It is because of disenchantment and low morale in the armed forces.

"Fred Akuffo himself condemned the former Head of State, General Acheampong, totally for his behavior and handling of affairs while in power. But what did he do? Stripping him of his military titles and benefits and calling him 'Mister'. Many people are suffering in Ghana. We are fed up!

"We see people who have amassed fabulous and unimaginable wealth, thanks to General Acheampong. It seems only fair to the people of this country that General Mr. Acheampong should account for his ill-gotten and dishonestly acquired wealth.

"How could General Akuffo sit back and hand over power to the civilians without attending to this immediate problem...? And it wasn't as if Akuffo wasn't aware of the frustration and anger of the junior ranks and civilians about this lack of action...

"Please, try and refrain from reporting such terrible uninformed rubbish".

The writer of the editorial later said on **BBC** that he was surprised by the "unusual response both from people in Ghana and Ghanaians living in London."

He was rather quite honest to admit that his writing on Ghana had been superficial.

"I know from being a correspondent in Africa that the gap between what is said in the public here and the realities on the ground is often considerable."

But that was initial reaction to the popular uprising of June 4. It was not just the Armed Forces who were on trial. Flight Lieutenant Jerry John Rawlings was still the accused. To 10 million people conditioned for a return to a constitutional and civilian rule, the young 31-year old airman had a heavy task to accomplish, a patriotic duty to perform.

In a radio and television broadcast on the night of June 5, Captain Boakye Djan, spokesman, named Flt. Lt. J. J. Rawlings as Chairman of the Armed Forces Revolutionary Council. Other members of the Council were named as:

Major Mensah-Poku
Major Mensah-Gbedemah
Warrant Officer Class Two Obeng
Lance Corporal Gatsiko
Private Owusu Adu

Corporal Owusu Boateng
Staff-Sergeant Alex Adjei
Lieutenant-Commander Barnor

On the programme, Capt. Boakye Djan asked all soldiers in town except those on essential duties to return to the barracks. He warned against "lawlessness" and said that any reaction of lawlessness "will be ruthlessly crushed".

Speaking on the same programme, Flt. Lt. Rawlings said the action of last Monday was a reaction to the "unjustifiable hardships of the few years." He assured the Nation and the world at large that the AFRC "shall not pursue justice using the path of unjustifiable vengeance." But then all those found guilty "will pay the appropriate penalty." He warned against molesting senior officers and said that all the "clean, disciplined, dedicated radical and action-oriented soldiers" would be needed in the exercise to assist the Council in saving and restoring the integrity of the country.

A new era had indeed dawned.

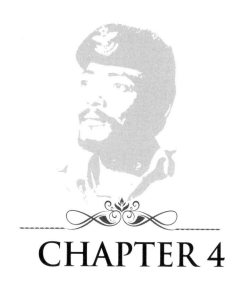

CHAPTER 4

THE CLEAN-UP OPERATION AND REACTIONS

Late April, 1979, it came to light at a committee investigating malpractices in the export of timber products that Major-General E. K. Utuka and Robert Ebenezer Abossey Kotei, both retired members of the Supreme Military Council (SMC) "issued chits to their favourites" to take away large quantities of lumber.

A witness told the Committee that the lumber, which was made up of 7,494 pieces of Odum and Wawa boards, were first impounded in September, 1976, when the Border Guards carried out special investigations at the border and "the lumber were seized and kept at TIMBOD's Depot at Aflao".

The witness, who was a Marketing Officer of the Timber Marketing Board (TIMBOD), said that TIMBOD later decided to sell the lumber to Togolese merchants *to earn foreign exchange for the country*. But before TIMBOD could communicate this to the

Government, the then Commanding Officer of the Aflao Border Guards came to TIMBOD Depot and supervised the loading of part of the consignment unto a Border Guard truck. This continued for a time.

Reports were made to the Government through the Border Guards Commander, Major-General Utuka, *but no action was taken*. The nation lost precious foreign exchange.

This is one of the few revelations which had come to light by June 4th. By the same time, it had been published that a Justice Amissah Committee set up to investigate external loans contracted between June, 1977 and July, 1978 by the Ministry of Finance had revealed certain improprieties on the part of General (Mr.) Kutu Acheampong who was then responsible for Finance. It had been found out that his personal interest in some of the agreements had led to heavy losses of foreign exchange to the country.

Mr. Acheampong's punishment: Not to hold any public office in Ghana.

One of the most drastic actions of the AFRC was the execution of eight top military officers, including the former Heads of State – Generals Kutu Acheampong, F. W. K. Akuffo and A. A. Afrifa. The only Commissioner of State with the group was Col. Roger Felli. The others were former SMC members, Major General E. K. Utuka, Major-General Robert Kotei, Rear Admiral Joy Kobla Amedume, and Air Vice-Marshall Yaw Boakye. They had been found guilty of corruption and abuse of office by a special court set up by the AFRC.

In Ghana, ordinary people rejoiced in drinking bars, and the University Campuses were thrown into excitement. The foreign media reported the first execution of Generals Acheampong and Utuka without any comment. It is significant to note that Acheampong was not a favourite of the West and therefore got no sympathy. A U.S. Foreign Office spokesman told the *Philadelphian Inquirer* that "it is a matter internal to Ghana."

In such circumstances, he commented, "the United States normally continues its diplomatic recognition of the new AFRC government."

That same day, Britain announced recognition of the new AFRC government.

Some famous words on General Acheampong's lips few days before his execution were "Nkrumah suffered the same fate, and I am not surprised it is happening to me…I cannot claim to be infallible. Perhaps my only fault was that I was too lenient."

Meanwhile, Acheampong had been alleged to have diverted 2 million dollars in government funds to buy houses abroad and distributed more than 4 million dollars among friends.

By this time, Ghana which once produced a third of the world's cocoa was recording only 20 per cent of world supplies. Inflation was running as high as 150 per cent a year, and the economy was on the verge of collapse.

Smuggling – a cause of Ghana's woes – was virtually legalized, with high Border Guard personnel freely authorizing it.

The *New York Times* of June 17 said of Acheampong:

"As Head of State, he presided over a period of corruption and economic hardship that saw the once prosperous West African State lose its influential role in regional affairs."

At the time Acheampong and Utuka were shot, some other senior military men had been arrested and were due to appear before the Special Court. What was not clear was whether the rest of the members of the Supreme Military Council would also face the firing squad. Speculation ran wild in town as soldiers chased hoarders and market women selling goods at prohibitive prices.

The elections fever soon died down; and while the politicians were actively planning their new roles in the next civilian government, the announcement was made that some more top officers had been found guilty of corruption and squandering of state funds.

A day after the execution of Acheampong, former British Overseas Development Minister, Judith Hart, had appealed to the AFRC Chairman to "spare the life of General Fred Akuffo".

Also, a group calling itself the African Bar Association had asked the AFRC to "protect fundamental human rights."

Flt. Lt. Rawlings told a *BBC* interviewer then that Ghana could not afford an "Iranian revolution", and that there was no need for any more executions.

The *NEWSWEEK* Magazine described Rawlings as "among the more moderate members of the new revolutionary council."

Stating that Rawlings was committed to handing over power to civilians, the magazine remarked:

"Radical, Marx-quoting junta members may not allow the new leader to keep even the deadline".

On 19th June, the **BBC** asked Rawlings if the AFRC did not impede transfer of power to civilians. The AFRC Chairman said: "No, I don't think so. I'll tell you what. What we are in a way trying to do is to give power back to the masses of this country.

"In other words, the masses should necessarily have the power, and the man at the top should only have the opportunity to serve us and do what is right…"

BBC: Isn't there going to be a terrible temptation for all of you on the AFRC if you see things going wrong again, say in a year or two's time, to intervene again?"

Rawlings said "No. If we should attempt to intervene again, at least I think we would have the moral justification to do so because we are trying to come back to barracks with clean hands. If we had come back to barracks as filthy as we had been or were, I would shoot the first military personnel who would ask us to intervene, no matter how corrupt the civilian government may be because I would consider it unfair and morally wrong".

One test would be if the AFRC men were going to go back to barracks with clean hands. The second would be if Dr. Limann was genuinely concerned about the suffering of the ordinary man – even to the point of his hopelessness.

As he Dr Limann himself said in an interview:

"If you go round the countryside, you see people who are completely indifferent to what is going on because they have lost hope…

"They have suffered for a long time and we the PNP do not believe we can ask them to suffer any more".

Dr Limann had just won the elections. He was quite optimistic, but then comes the news of 26th June: Six more executions by firing squad, including two former leaders Generals Akuffo and Afrifa. Mrs. Margaret Thatcher was the first to react after the U.S. She expressed her "abhorrence" to the executions and said that Britain had been in touch with other members of the European Economic Community, the U.S. and Canada about joint representations to the Ghana Government.

At this time, the U.S. was more concerned about the situation in the Nicaragua where the revolutionary Sandinista forces were forcing President Somoza to relinquish power. The war had moved into Managua, the capital, and the Sandinistas, through their Provisional Government, had rejected American proposals for a ceasefire and relief aid. It was left for Britain, former colonial matron, to handle the Ghana case.

What one may call a fair assessment of the feeling in Accra was heard on the British Broadcasting Corporation Programme *24 hours* on June 27, from a correspondent just returning to London from Accra, Andrew Walker. He said in answer to a question:

"Well, I think if it had been left to Flt. Lt. Rawlings, there wouldn't have been any more executions…But he has been under enormous pressure. You see, the AFRC, of which he is the Chairman, consists mainly of what we call other ranks, the NCOs, Lance Corporals and a Private. The great pressure has come from these ranks…and they feel that if they can't punish the people whom they think have brought the country to such wretched stage…they're going to get off scot-free again because future governments would probably linger on this issue or send them to prison or confiscate their assets or both…

"And so these people, and I think *this attitude is also among civilians*, not only soldiers – these people say we must punish them severely for what they have done to Ghana".

As expected, the Western countries protested to the AFRC while the Eastern ones watched "with keen interest". Representations were also made by the Nigerian Government, which was supplying a bulk of Ghana's crude oil, Ivory Coast, Togo and Upper Volta.

On **Network Africa**, another correspondent was saying that when she left Accra everybody was expecting more executions; and she added:

"It has come as no surprise to me personally and I'm sure to many Ghanaians".

But *Ghanaians dislike bloodshed* and it is not the Ghanaian way of doing things. Ghana had not had a history of shedding blood. However, as the correspondent said, "Many people feel this is why

Ghana had suffered most in the last three years because people do not expect to account for their action in the way. The students at the universities are demanding blood and there have been slogans at all parts of the campuses asking for more blood but..."

Asked whether she thought majority of Ghanaian were in favour of the executions, the correspondent replied that among the young people, the general impression was that they were in favour. Of course, the old generation and the middle-class were not happy.

Nigeria soon announced that she was stopping delivery of oil in protest against the executions.

What was the local reaction?

The articulate and dynamic student body, the National Union of Ghana Students, was among the many progressive organisations which condemned the foreign remarks on the execution:

"We condemn in the strongest terms the threats allegedly issued by the Obasanjo Government in Nigeria to cut off supplies to Ghana. The clean-up exercise here has set a new precedent in African politics...The pleas of the Paris-teleguided governments in Ivory Coast, Togo and Upper Volta also show the depth of their hypocrisy and how unfair they have been to the suffering people of Ghana. When our timber, cocoa, diamond, rice, maize and essential imported commodities were being smuggled to these countries by the few local enemies of the people of Ghana these "good neighbours" of ours actively collaborated with them. And now that the inexorable arm of the revolution wants to exact justice on these culprits, they dare plead for mercy for them...!"

Three days later, Flt. Lt Rawlings went on radio and television to say that there would be no more executions. Instead "we shall resort to such forms of punishment as confiscation of illegally acquired wealth and imprisonment terms of productive labour".

From Europe, the Overseas Branch of the Nation Union of Ghana Students supported the executions as "justified" and suggested that the cleaning operation should not be limited only to corrupt personalities of the Armed Forces of Ghana, but "it must also be extended to their civilian counterparts engaged in trade, commerce, industry, administration and management."

The students also suggested that both retired and new party leaders should be subjected to probing.

It was also the view of the students that the AFRC should carry on with its intention of "sweeping away the filth of corruption and never pay heed to the protests of certain foreign states, powers (like the U.S.A., Britain and West Germany) and international organizations against the executions".

Then, like the feeling of progressives at home, the point was made that "such institutions and countries never protest when Ghanaian masses suffer and die of squalor, disease, hunger and abject poverty…"

The Ghana Muslims Representative Council also sent a message of support to the AFRC for the Council's ability "in dispensing justice promptly and inflicting the just and due penalty without fear or favour". The Council welcomed the decision of the AFRC to dispatch those found guilty from now on to Penal Farms and confiscate their properties instead of imposing the death penalty which should be "reserved for those who commit murder".

Despite the fact that the AFRC was determined to relinquish power to those elected on 18th June, there was still a large degree of skepticism in the elite camp. For the working masses, the boldness with which the AFRC had dealt with untouchables in the society was a rare feat. They were even more impressed with the lowering of prices in the market and the increase in the producer price of cocoa. If Jerry Rawlings had stood elections at this time, he would easily have won without sweat. Yet the process towards handing over had already been initiated.

An elite group, the Society for National Welfare, reacted even more sharply to the international concerns. They issued a press release which said:

"The Society for National Welfare wishes to express concern about some aspects of the international reactions to current events in Ghana, in particular the use or the threat to use economic and other sanctions to influence internal policies and decisions.

"While we do not deny any nation, individual or organization the freedom to make observations on and react to events in other countries, we note with very grave concern the extremely hostile reactions to recent events in Ghana from our traditional friends in Africa, in the Commonwealth and some other parts of the world. Some of these reactions seem to be aimed at deflecting the Armed Forces Revolutionary Council (AFRC) from its stated objective, namely that of cleaning up the country of those vices which have resulted in the almost impossible living conditions to which the majority of Ghanaians have been subjected within the last few years.

"What is even more disappointing in these reactions is the almost total lack of appreciation of the circumstances that led to the action of June 4th. And yet most of the countries have been aware of the depths to which our country had sunk as a result of the rapacity, corruption and extreme insensitivity of those who had taken up arms ostensibly to redeem Ghanaians from the intolerable conditions under which they were living. Ghana became the laughing-stock of the world, and we were even openly ridiculed in a television quiz programme of a sister African country. As a result of these intolerable conditions, large numbers of our professionals, graduate teachers, mechanics and other able-bodied young people, out of sheer frustration, left to seek their fortunes in neighbouring countries.

"Deprivation became almost total; basic commodities could not be obtained, except at astronomical prices and after hours of waiting in queue. Hospitals were without drugs and spare parts were unobtainable. People had to travel to neighbouring countries to buy basic things like soap, toilet paper, sugar, toothpaste, cooking oil, basic medicines, spare parts, tyres, etc. This situation inevitably gave rise to a flourishing black market which further eroded the value of our currency, the cedi. The cost of living was increasing by the day, and when the basic minimum wage was ¢4.00 a day, a member of the last Government lamented openly that one needed ¢15.00 to get a single meal.

"All these were happening at a time when cocoa, our major foreign exchange earner, and other exports like gold and timber were fetching very high prices on the world market. This was the major question the students and professionals were asking from May 1977 when the needles suffering forced them to strikes, beginning a series of industrial actions in reaction to the prevailing intolerable circumstances.

"In this wide sea of poverty, hardships and deprivation, there arose at the same time islands of flamboyant affluence and conspicuous consumption in the state. Mansions were being put up by people in government and by the new crop of spurious businessmen who had been issued with import licences. The gap between those who had and those who had not grew wider, and since most people could not survive on their meagre wages, they resorted to all manner of dubious stratagems to survive.

"The Union/National Government idea which was put up as a sort of diversion did not make people forget the stark realities of life. Reports in local and foreign papers during the period spoke of the deteriorating conditions of life in the country. Morale was consequently low, productivity decreased and the downward slide continued. With Acheampong's removal in July 1978, an opportunity was gained to correct the situation, but because of their complicity in the shameless plunder of the national coffers, his successors sat by helplessly and offered a political palliative to the people by rescinding the decision on Union/Government.

"It had become clear that the cause of our problems was flagrant corruption, and blatant abuse of office, and that something had to be done about it, if we were to lay a healthy foundation for national development. This is the justification for the action of June 4th.

"We are aware of the concern that has been expressed in international circles about the methods being used and severity of punishment meted out. We do concede that procedures adopted so far have not met the expected standards. But our friends are certainly not unaware that various bodies in Ghana, including the Society for National Welfare, have rightly expressed concern about this. In one of our early statements, we called for the scrupulous observance of the principles of natural justice and fundamental human rights in the trials.

"In subsequent statement issued on 28/6/79, we observed 'we note with regret that there has been no information given to the public about the (membership) of this court and how it operates, but the rapidity with which cases have been disposed of leaves room for very serious misgivings'. We, however, recall with gratification that the AFRC have, to some degree, positively reacted to this concern.

"In the light of the above, we think it will more helpful if those now contemplating the use of economic and other sanctions against Ghana would take note of the following: the basic purpose of the actions of the Government is to help eradicate the sort of corruption, abuse of office and exploitation which have been rampant in Ghana, and indeed in several developing countries, and which constitute the most serious obstacle in equitable and sustained socio-economic development.

"In this atmosphere of corruption and abuse of office, domestic resources are utilized well below optimum, foreign technical and other aid is wasted or diverted to private accounts, and social stability is jeopardized.

"It is needless to stress that under such conditions, no nation can be assured of a stable, peaceful and prosperous future. The house-cleaning exercise as the Government has stated is therefore partly meant to ensure that aid and credit provided to the country are used for the purpose for which they are granted, that is, for the benefit and development of the whole population.

"We are all naturally concerned about civic rights, but the present Ghanaian situation must also be judged in its world-wide context, especially in the light of current social events in several other developing countries. The root causes of these upheavals can be found in the absence of probity and accountability in public life in these countries. We therefore, expect that our detractors, as well as friends would, through their own actions and otherwise, address themselves a little more to the question of probity in public life, and help us to achieve this goal.

"Our creditors and other friends who now seem to be over-reacting and cutting credit and withdrawing their goodwill may soon discover that they are only contributing to chaos and total collapse of law and order in the country. Neither they nor Ghana could benefit from this eventually.

"We, therefore, hope that our traditional suppliers and creditors will maintain existing commercial and economic links."

ISSUED BY THE COUNCIL, SOCIETY FOR NATIONAL WELFARE
(Sgd) NANA WEREKO AMPEM
(Sgd) E. S. AIDOO
President
Vice-President

In my research for material for this book, I stumbled upon a letter sent by a group of students from the University of Ghana to J. J. Rawlings, dated 7th July, 1979. It said in part:

"We are grateful to you and all members of the AFRC. We congratulate you and give you our total and unconditional moral, spiritual support for the achievement and the triumphant objectives of the revolution.

"You have entered the political scene just at the time when the country needed a radical and courageous leader of your caliber. We salute this historical event, and hope you will transform this country into a new, rich strong and prosperous society.

"We note with satisfaction that all your revolutionary actions are aimed at alleviating the suffering of the working class from the exploitation by the greedy and unpatriotic Ghanaians…"

"You are the Fidel Castro of Ghana. The fire of revolution which you have already sparked shall continue to burn after you, and for future generations…
"The revolution must continue, in all directions – political, economic, social, cultural, agricultural, scientific and technical – without interruption…So any attempt to hand over political power to the bourgeoisie will simply mean the failure of our revolution and the betrayal of working class..."

Such sentiments were rife among the student population, but the AFRC seemed committed to its programme.

CHAPTER 5

THE ELECTION FESTIVAL

On Sunday, 13th May, 1979, the Catholic hierarchy of Ghana caused to be read in all the churches what was called a joint pastoral letter. The ban on political activities had been lifted and as many as 20 Parties had declared their intention to contest.

"We know that Ghanaians have been, as it were, groping in the dark", the statement admitted. "We have been living in difficult, indeed abnormal circumstances. *The evidence is there for all to see that our country's economy has virtually collapsed, that morale is low, and that we seem to have lost most of our cherished moral values.*"

The clergy provided the analysis of the situation:

"Most Ghanaians would agree that one of the root causes of our economic problems is the unscrupulous behavior of those whose task it is to ensure that goods reach the people in reasonable quantities and at fair prices".

But then went on to point out that: "If commodities cannot be imported into the country it is because too many persons at all levels of the administration *have misdirected the available foreign currency*".

Referring to hoarding and sale of commodities at exhorbitant prices, the Catholic hierarchy reminded the congregations: "*And we all know what Christ himself thought of and did to the changers and traders in the temple*".

The clergymen noted that "*money and property seem to be the only measure* of a person's worth and standing in our society *irrespective of how he acquired them.* This situation has brought about the moral decay we see around us…"

In conclusion, the Catholic top men said rather lamely: "In this situation, the preparations being made to return to *constitutional normalcy* such as the work of the Constituent Assembly, the formation of political parties and the orderly electoral campaign we have had so far, *give reasons for hope*".

The Catholic hierarchy was not the only one group which hoped that the return to party politics would solve all the problems of the country. The Ghana Bar Association, the Professional Bodies Association, and the Christian Council of Ghana were all waiting frantically for the elections to usher in a civilian administration.

Of course, the seven years of military rule had been a failure. The economy had been recklessly handled, the *survival of the fittest* had become the order of the day and the gap between the haves and the have-nots had widened. But what was probably even sadder was that the senior military leadership who had taken power "to redeem" the people had been busy amassing wealth and property. So that the only apparent alternative was the handover of power to civilian leaders.

But then why did the Catholic clergy think that they could not recommend some "clean, honest" and "morally upright" persons to Ghanaians? Or, for that matter, why didn't the Church give support to one Party or group of people?

At some point the Catholic Bishop of Kumasi, Rt. Rev. Akwasi Sarpong, when contacted if he would be a Presidential candidate, said, "Personally I do not feel I'm competent for such a post...We as priests must stick to our profession".

So, the church hierarchy forfeited their right and freedom to participate actively in the government of the people by the people. The rest of the civilian population were watching. But, at the end of the day, the Parties were formed in the capitals and the rural areas became recipient of the news.

The nearest to the clergy forming a party was Mr. William Ofori-Atta, a veteran politician and statesman-turned preacher who brought together a blend of new and old faces to found the **United National Convention.**

A harvest of political parties was anticipated.

When the lifting of the ban on party politics was announced the race for power was swift, and the mass media abandoned the problems of the masses and used their pages to cover press conferences of politicians.

One Dr. Owusu Ansah announced that a **People's Freedom Party** was going to be formed, its main objective being to "create a scientific socialist state based on the philosophical ideals of the late Osagyefo Dr. Kwame Nkrumah and the indigenous values of the Ghanaian society". That was probably the last time Ghanaians heard of that Party.

Then came the news from Dr. Ackah Blay-Miezah's camp: "the Oman Ghana Trust Holding Limited may go into politics…in a bid to restore a definite and stable political climate to guarantee the safety of its huge economic investment". (***Daily Graphic***, December 30, 1978)

This intention surfaced in the formation of the **People's Vanguard Party** led by Dr. Ackah Blay-Miezah. Following Dr Blay-Miezah's conviction in court, Kwesi Amoako-Atta stepped in the leader's shoes. But few weeks before the elections, the Party withdrew and its few members filed behind other parties.

The formation of parties itself is a very curious game. With clear aims of satisfying selfish convictions, parties emerge, only to disintegrate when finances are hard to come by or when power struggle sets in.

One morning, the press reported that a group of youth leaders, lawyers and statesmen had decided to form a political party. The statement issued named some of the leaders as Nana Okutwer Bekoe, Alhaji Ismaila, Dr. E. V. C. De-Graft Johnson and Fr. Frank Boret. The priorities of the Party would be "to restore rationality and efficiency in the administration of the nation's resources and finances…"

But, then, hanging over the heads of most prospective politicians was the Disqualification Decree 1979 which sought to ban certain individuals from holding public office as a result of their past demeanours. Yet other Ghanaians were fed up with the old politicians.

Headlines like:

The Old Politicians Must Leave the Scene! began to appear. New names started showing up. L. Oteng-Gyang told a press conference that the **Liberty Party** of the 2nd Republic had been re-christened the **New Generation Party** to "reform the economic mess in which the country finds itself".

Col. Frank Bernasko (Rtd) also announced that the **Action Party** was being formed.

In Accra, Mr. Osei Poku, a journalist, registered the **Democratic People's Party of Ghana** saying that it would establish "a firm revolutionary base by maintaining the complete unity of the nation and safe-guard by all means possible the independence, sovereignty and territorial integrity of Ghana".

Mr. Justice Edrah, a business executive, also declared the formation of the "**Development Filosofas Kongress**".

Then came Mr. Kwaku Oppong, Planning Officer of the Building and Road Research Institute in Kumasi. His Party was to be called **Young People's Front**. He said his Party believed that the youth of the country should be jerked from what he termed "their Rip-Van-Winklish slumber and get involved in activities within their horizons".

From Kumasi again, Dr. John Bilson, a private Medical Practitioner, launched his **Third Force Party**, asking Ghanaians to reject the old politicians. One of his first promises to the electorate was: "We will pay the farmers the world cocoa price".

Far away in London, Dr. Francis Yanney, a Ghanaian Economics lecturer, formed the **Ghanaian Common People's Party**. Not much was heard of him again.

Mr. K. D. Mensah called a press conference in Accra and announced the formation of the **National Conciliation Party** which he said would build "a classless society".

J. Evans Anfom said he would lead a party to be known as the **Gold Coasters Party.** The Party would "encourage chieftaincy, organize a socialist state and do the will of the majority'".

Of course the old guards of the **Convention People's Party** (CPP) gathered together to form the **People's National Party**. Alhaji Imoru Egala, one time Minister in the Nkrumah regime, was the leader.

But some of the CPP old guards wanted to form their own parties. Mr. Johnny S. F. Hansen, a barrister-at-law and former leader of the People's Popular Party, formed the **People's Revolutionary Army** "to combat the negative forces of imperialism, neo colonialism, fascism, semi-feudalism, bureaucratic capitalism and all forms of oppression, deprivation and exploitation".

Mr. H. S. T. Provencal, also of the Nkrumah guard, announced the **Ghana National Party** with a pledge to "uphold the ideals, philosophy and teachings of the late Dr. Kwame Nkrumah".

Prof. Mawuse Dake launched the **National Democratic Front** to be sponsored by the Trade Union Congress. Interim Chairman was Dr. E. V. C. De-Graft Johnson.

The Welfare Party was also announced by a lawyer, Dr. Isaac Ephson, who said the party would change the name of Ghana to Gold Coast and "make education free for all from elementary to University level...and also let workers own their own houses".

Party politics is an interesting phenomenon. The women wanted to be heard. So, Miss Regina Asamany, former Minister in the Nkrumah regime, launched the **Mother Ghana Solidarity Party** to "ensure women have equal opportunities in taking decisions on vital national issues".

Other Parties were later out-doored: The **New Nation Party** led by Mr. Mark Diamond Nii Addy. The **Ghana United Movement** led by Mr. Imoru Ayarna. Lacking any popular base and probably the resources, the two leaders later stood as independent candidates.

Mr. Kwaku Boateng was to be leader of the **United Liberal Party** and Dr. Ephraim Amu was leading the **Patriotic Alliance**. George Osei founded the **Reformed People's Party**, with Mr. Kwame Nyanteh as a leading Member, but Mr. Nyanteh was soon to be seen as an independent Presidential candidate. Kwabena Adomako Mensah's **Citizens Forward Party** did not see much light.

It is important to note the modus by which parties are formed because of the lessons that the future will be called upon to enumerate. There was one particular case in Tamale which is worth narrating:

One day was set aside for a meeting of the Northern Youth Association, an elite grouping of youthful citizens from the Northern and Upper Regions. The purpose was to discuss a report from a five member committee which had been commissioned to find out which of the big parties in the south could be backed by the Association to win the elections.

The Committee recommended two parties, the PNP and the PFP, but this signaled a division of the ranks of the Association.

Then, all of a sudden, one member, Alhaji Abubakar Al-Hassan, emerged with a proposal that they should form a party to be known as the **Social Democratic Party**. Apparently, he had done some homework on this, so by popular acclamation the motion was accepted. An interim executive was nominated with Alhaji Alhassan himself as leader, Col. Roger Felli, Alhaji Ibrahim Mahami, Mrs Hawa Ayabo and others, as members.

Later, other youth members present declared support for other parties but Alhaji Alhassan's strategy later earned him a Parliamentary seat for the same Party which was being launched in Accra with the sponsorship of the Trades Union Congress and led by a countryman, Alhaji Ibrahim Mahama.

Alliances changed as quickly as the speed of a motion film picture and without clear perception of ideological positions. Politicians crossed carpets, some depending on which side was the highest bidder or hottest favourite.

What was fascinating were some of the headline promises and pledges:

No more poverty – says Blay Miezah
ACP: **We'll End All Coups d'états**
Stop Destroying Opponents' Posters – N. Addy
PFP: **We'll Ensure Absolute Freedom**
We'll Save the Poor – PRP
ACP Will Guarantee Farmers' Loans
PNP Will Wipe All Traces of Tribalism
"Give me a Chance" – Bernasko
Vote for New Faces – ACP
UNC: **We'll Improve Common Man's Lot**
We shall be Frugal – Third Force
Disregard Vain Promises – Addy
We'll Cultivate Afram Plains – UNC

By 6th March, 1979, 16 out of the numerous parties had fulfilled conditions set by the Political Parties Decree, 1979. Some of those who had faded out either lacked the political determination or popular base or else had no funds to continue.

It is significant to note that, though Ghanaians had been conditioned to prepare for the elections as a panacea to the country's problems, the party leaders at some point thought they needed more time.

Certainly, given less than six months to canvass for votes imposed a very big task on the organisers of the parties and, at some point, they must have weighed their capacity against the current trends.

THE ELECTION FESTIVAL

By March 21st, 1979, **The People's National Party**, said to be the offspring of Nkrumah's Convention People's Party, had nominated Mr. Imoru Egala as Presidential Candidate. A week later, leaders of the then 16 Parties met General Akuffo to discuss a few vital issues. Thirteen out of 16 Parties asked that the date for the handover should be extended from July 1st to January 1980. They also asked that the deadline for payment and registration of candidates should be extended, meaning also that the date for the elections should be pushed further. As Dr. Ephraim Amu, leader of the **Patriotic Alliance** said: "It looks as if everything is being done in a rush".

Indeed, the populace was anxious to see an end to military rule; and the Supreme Military Council was equally in a hurry to return to barracks or retire with the attendant constitutional immunities and the wealth acquired.

So General Akuffo could only say "We do not want to change the date fixed for handing over. We serve the Nation and as soldiers it must be the entire Nation which should say that we should stay on. We, on our own, cannot change the date".

A newspaper comment summed it all up in the editorial column headed: **They Beat the Retreat**.
"Surprisingly some Ghanaian political leaders are beating the retreat just when the country is well on the road to civilian rule.

Even some professionals who asked Acheampong regime to step down last year are now bidding for time, virtually appealing to the SMC not to hand over power until they have completed their 'homework'.

"'The homework' we know, is nothing but the fact that some parties can't sort things out – they are all fighting for leadership posts.

"And yet the noisiest group of people calling for an end to military rule are the same politicians who now want to retire to their corners.

"We do not want to assume that the noise was coming from empty barrels loaded only with air".

(**Daily Graphic**, March 30, 1979)

Earlier, at the same meeting, Mr. Imoru Egala had asked that the SMC should not issue out decrees to disqualify prospective candidates in the coming elections. He said the Government should allow the electorate the free hand to disqualify candidates.

Why was Imoru Egala scared of the Disqualification Decree?

Anyhow, two days later, the SMC enacted the Disqualification Decree, and Imoru Egala was out of the race. The Central Committee of the People's National Party, the same group which elected Imoru Egala, convened an emergency meeting.

By the next morning, an unknown Dr. Hilla Limann had been selected to be Presidential Candidate. Some said that Dr. Limann had earlier in the party games been mentioned as a potential parliamentary candidate for the contesting Popular Front Party because of his close relationship with Dr. Safo Adu of the PFP.

This time, because the Party was bent on tilting the balance of the political power in favour of the people of the north of Ghana, Imoru Egala was virtually given the mandate to propose an alternative candidate. His nomination was Dr. Hilla Limann, born at Gwolu in the Sisala District in the Upper Region.

He was a Foreign Service Officer holding a degree in Political Science and a Diploma in French Language and Civilization. His Doctorate degree was in Constitutional Law.

Out of the 16 Parties, only six finally qualified to contest the elections.

These were the:
  (1)   People's National Party (PNP)
  (2)   Popular Front Party (PFP)
  (3)   Action Congress Party (ACP)
  (4)   Third Force Party (TFP)
  (5)   United National Convention (UNC)
  (6)   Social Democratic Front(SDF)

There were four other Independent candidates who wanted to be President: Dr. R. P. Baffour, Ahaji Imoru Ayarna, Mr. Kwame Nyanteh and Nii Diamond Mark Addy.

Even when it was known that the economy had collapsed, these Parties did not cease making wild promises.

For example, Mr. Kwame Nyanteh, an independent Presidential candidate, declared one day that a few months after his election, he would take steps *to hold a referendum for Ghanaians to adopt a national language.*

But then, the Armed Forces Revolutionary Council was firmly in power. There were even doubts over whether the elections would be held at all.

On the eve of Election Day, Flt. Lt. J.J. Rawlings, Chairman of the AFRC, went on air and appealed to Ghanaians to go out and vote.

Less than 40 per cent of the eligible voters went out to vote and the results were released as follows:

PNP won 71 out of the 140 seats
PFP 42 seats
UNC 13 seats
ACP 10 seats
SDF 3 seats

The Third Force Party failed to win any seat, but an independent candidate, Mr. Harry Sawyer obtained a seat.

For the Presidential, Dr. Hilla Limann of PNP won the second round with 1,118,305 votes against Mr. Victor Owusu of PFP.

It is not immediately available how much each of the political heavyweights invested in the election campaigns but this is open to easy conjecture. Most of the young candidates for Parliament had no means of funding, so they had to rely on businessmen, particularly road contractors; well-to-do lawyers, who were later found not to have been paying taxes, sponsored a number of candidates.

In the PNP, it was an open secret that the Presidential Candidate, Dr. Hilla Limann had no money, being a "poor Civil Servant." The heavyweights, like Nana Okutwer Bekoe, had to fund his campaign trail.

.

One interesting aspect of the whole deceit and illusion associated with party elections came to light in one of the dailies later:

"The Bernasko Cutlass"

"The Government has been called upon to investigate how the leader of the ACP, Col. Frank Bernasko, came by a large consignment of cutlasses which he is alleged to have distributed to the electorate of the Tarkwa-Aboso Constituency on the eve of last Friday's bye elections…

"When contacted, Col. Bernasko said he bought the cutlasses from the Crocodile Matchets Factory and gave eight cartons to the Western Region.
"He stated, if the PNP is complaining because I distributed cutlasses, what of the mackerel, sugar and moneys they also gave out?"

(***Ghanaian Times***, November 20 1979)

No honest Party can deny that cutlasses, sugar, mackerel, monies were distributed to the poor electorate, most of them farmers, to influence them to vote in their favour.

Answering questions later on this system, Flt. Lt. Rawlings commented:

"If we say total justice, that is exactly what I mean. When can the poor villager reason for himself and without any influence determine who is honest enough to be selected to present his views?

"When you are talking of freedom and justice, you don't mean it for only those crafty, opportunistic and double-tongued cheats, do you?"

CHAPTER 6

THE TEST OF A HAND-OVER

Questions that Flt. Lt. J. J. Rawlings had to answer particularly from the Western news media included:

"You were quoted as saying that what Ghana needed was a strong man who would be a benevolent dictator. Do you really mean that?"

Or

"Aren't these politicians who have been selected today and so forth going to be terribly nervous, be looking over their shoulder?"

To the first, he replied:

"By that I mean by we needed a very strong man, I mean definitely, a very disciplined man with a very willing and generous magnanimity to be able to look at situations from another man's point of view instead of always having to look at situations from his very own personal point of view - but just don't waiver, stay strong, don't be corrupted."

To the second, he said:

"I suppose so, but what have you to fear if you haven't committed any offence…"

In answer to another, he stressed:

"I don't know what it means to be a Socialist – as is referred to in the Eastern countries, or a communist or a capitalist. What I do recognize is that my men, my batman or soldier down there, has his worth; I mean, he is just as important as I am. Without him, my shoes won't be polished; my dishes wouldn't be washed; my uniforms wouldn't be washed. I would be dirty and filthy and I would have to take time off my work to do all these chores, you know…"

Interviewed as the results of the election were being counted, Flt. Lt. Jerry Rawlings said he intended to remain in the Armed Forces after handing over power to a civilian government.

"I intend to remain in the Forces in the same humble position as I was before," he said.

The humility of Rawlings was a known factor. Two Brigadiers whom I talked to confirmed that it was his "discipline and humility" that endeared him to most of his own Senior Officers.

"And he is quite a sincere person", Squadron Leader B. K. said.

But behind his humility and sincerity there was a growing fear in the Western Press that he might not keep his word over the handover promise.

Originally, the handover date was scheduled for October 1, but when it was realized it would coincide with the same event in neighbouring Nigeria, it was shifted to September 24.

Anxiety was quite high and the PNP was particularly expectant. "We didn't sleep that night", one of Dr. Limann's Press secretaries told me. "We stayed up in his office in the State House and prepared four speeches, going to bed early the next morning. This is because he kept changing phrases and words in his speeches. You know, Dr. Limann was quite meticulous."

This was the last day of the AFRC in power. Their 'Revolution of Social Conscience' was changing guards, the men who took arms to restore value of accountability and selflessness were leaving the scene. It was ominous, though, their last message to the Nation; as Flt. Lt. Rawlings warned:

"No one should mistake the sweeping force and dynamic energy of our Revolution of Social Conscience."

The television camera shifted from one AFRC member to another as Flt. Lt. Rawlings, in a very solemn tone said:

"Time ticks away fast and with each passing minute our brief administration comes to its close.

"We have no regrets.

"We appear before you humbly to share with you these sentiments which constitute our final will and testament…"

Flt. Lt. Rawlings took a short breath, looked at the faces of his colleagues, as if asking for final consent, and muttered:

"*We go back to our vocation in the Armed Forces*, ready to work to assist the in-coming Government from our modest positions…We make our exit and trust God that our Revolution of Social Conscience may serve as a propitious wind to sail the Ship of State to a safe and new haven of political stability. Good Night. *Long Live the Revolution.*"

How many politicians understood the full import of those words? To many, it was "good riddance." The shake-up in the society had been far-reaching. The boys had cleansed the country of "the national pollution." Their limited task was to cleanse the Armed Forces which "had lost its bearings in the wilderness of indiscipline and unprofessional behavior." But of long-term significance was the aim to "launch a Revolution which *would cleanse the Nation, direct the hearts and mind of our people against injustices and restructure ultimately the pattern of our national life.*"

The 112 days of the AFRC had exposed greed, lust for power and "the wicked use of power to entrench privilege among a few in the society."

As Rawlings said, "It was as though by some malign act of Providence, Ghana had achieved independent statehood only to be held to ransom by a succession of selfish individuals."

For most politicians, power was sweet. The grandeur of riding in a new car, chauffeur-driven and taking decision for the people in Parliament! Or making long speeches at a rally to be cheered intermittently!

But there were others, sincerely seeking an opportunity to serve the people.

The short regime of the AFRC was poised to set standards – to sharpen social conscience, *setting in motion a movement of ideas* which would "henceforth militate actively against the politics and morality of wealth and privilege which had gripped our national life."

Rawlings admitted that the results had not shown. "We cannot help but feel that we only scratched the bare surface of our national problems. It would take time, immense effort and determination to see viable results."

The AFRC, as has been said, had set standards. Rawlings gave an account of their performance in a radio and television broadcast: "*We did not seek laurels and trophies*, let none do. We did not seek the exercise of naked power, let none betray the ultimate source of power; we did not seek to divide the country; let none do".

At no time did Rawlings forget to acknowledge the source of their power – the masses. "The Revolution was carried through not by us here" (meaning other AFRC members). "No! Indeed the revolutionaries are among you the several millions of our compatriots…With equal gratitude we acknowledge the enthusiastic support and dedication which we enjoyed from the ordinary man in the street".

The next morning – 24th September 1979 – the precincts of the Parliament House was crowded by 8:00 a.m. Invited guests with Cards were allowed into the main hall, but outside the building were thousands of people from all walks of life. It was a historic moment. Tears were falling, fingers were snapping, sweat was drenching bodies, and the sun was beautifully brightening the talking drums and colourful kente cloth of the National Folkloric Group, sapping their energies in meaningful vibrations!

The military landrover which brought in AFRC members stole the show. The people mobbed it and cheered wildly as Flt. Lt. Rawlings gave them all a salute.

President-elect Dr. Hilla Limann was gorgeously dressed in kente-woven "batakari". Inside Parliament House, the cameras flicked and the cheers neutralized the solemnity of the occasion.

Six weeks before, 10th August, while inaugurating the joint commission of the in-coming administration, Rawlings had hoped that "the commission will make it possible for the Armed Forces and the Nation in general to rest assured that the moral revolution that has been initiated since June 4th will not die away with the departure of the AFRC."

He had added: "If the slightest indication were to be given that the new administration would put out the flames of moral regeneration lit by the AFRC, it would demoralize the Nation and bring about untold confusion."

Dr Limann was too intelligent not to have misunderstood the warning. But he also had his own intellectual arrogance which definitely would dismiss such "empty threats". His style of government and his concept of constitutional administration were totally different. He had read of revolutions in books but it was a different thing having the strength and capacity to carry on with a process that had been started without his participation.

Yet, Flt. Lt. J.J. Rawlings had even more compelling and historic words billed for the handing over ceremony. He told the attentive Parliament:

"To you, Mr. President, your Government and members of this Honourable House, we of the AFRC, in the light of our reading of the situation, make a fervent appeal never to lose sight of this new consciousness of the Ghanaian people. Never before have the eyes of so many been focused on so few, Mr. President. The few are you, the illustrious members of our new civilian administration. The many are those in the factories and on the farms, in the dormitories and junior quarters, who will be watching you, with eagles' eyes to see whether the change they are hoping for will actually materialize in their life."

The AFRC had seized buildings, motor vehicles, factories, farms, money in banks, physical cash and company shares, worth millions of Cedis which were acquired 'through corrupt means'.

The revolutionary government had also managed to collect hundreds of millions of cedis in taxes which organizations and individuals owed to the state and which they did not want to pay.

All these corrupt practices and many more had made the masses aware that their suffering need not have reached the terrible extent they had reached in recent years.

J. J. Rawlings put it more candidly:

"It has been forcibly brought home to all our people that while they were starving because food prices were high, while they risked death on falling sick because drugs were in short supply, while they were paying exorbitant rents and while they were dejected and despondent because of the intolerable heights to which inflation in the country had generally risen, there were others in the society who were dipping their hands freely into the Nation's coffers so that they and their families could live in the opulence of conspicuous consumption".

As the loudspeakers outside Parliament House blared these words, ordinary Ghanaians nodded their heads, naturally expecting that the new civilian administration would be equally concerned.

"I am sure also, Mr. President, that all the work that we have not had time to do will be carried out by your Government", Rawlings told Limann.

The last bit of the out-going AFRC Chairman's speech went deep down the hearts of the new President and the Honourable Ministers and Members of Parliament who looked at Rawlings with keen eyes:

"We wish you good luck... That you did not chicken out of the election but went ahead to seek representation of your people in spite of the fact that we were on the scene, with plain evidence of our revolutionary intent, suggests that you are men of mettle.

"GHANA IS LOOKING UP TO YOU", Rawlings said in conclusion.

The thunderous applause was spontaneous. Rawlings and the AFRC had made their last official statement. History was being made as Rawlings handed over the scroll of office to Dr. Limann. After Limann's inaugural address, Flt. Lt. John Jerry Rawlings, followed by Capt. Boakye Djan, joined the platoon outside to salute the new President. Shouts of "J.J.", "J.J.", rocked the Parliament House building and sent vibrations and echoes far into the atmosphere.

"...It was this need for change that caused Ghanaians to embrace the principal objectives of the PNP manifesto; objectives which seem to be re-echoed in the motives behind the June 4 Revolution now considered by many as a necessary soul-searching, self-cleansing operation in this period of crisis of confidence and conscience."

Dr. Limman went on to say:

"This operation, therefore, sets a pattern which the Third Republic shall have to follow to its logical conclusions".

The crowd in Parliament House and outside applauded when he added:

"**The measures initiated by the AFRC must lead to continuous progress of the aspiration of all Ghanaians and not just make another phase of temporary expediency after**

which we may relapse into the same old ways which have destroyed our economy and our image as a people. There can be no turning back..."

In fact, this was not the first time he had promised not to set the clock back. He had pledged much earlier that he would "not entertain any petition for the reversal of AFRC actions against corrupt elements."

And, indeed, Limann had legal support from the decree which had become part of the law of the land:

"It shall not be lawful for any Court to entertain any action or proceedings whatsoever for the purpose of questioning any decision, judgement, findings, order or proceedings of any Special Court convened under Section1 of the Decree; and for the removal of doubts, it shall not be lawful for any Court to entertain any application for an order or writ in the nature of habeas corpus, certiorari, mandamus, prohibition or quo warranto and declaration in respect of any decision."

The Transitional Provisions enshrined in the Constitution, and worked out by both the AFRC and the PNP gave blessing to these declarations.

Was it just the change into Presidential robes that enamoured Hilla Limann?

For it did not take too long for him to abandon the "revolutionary rhetoric" of continuing with the clean-up exercise.

Of course, Limann had the constitutional power but not the authority. The authority was to come from the "old guards" who had pushed him upwards. And then the pressure was to come from a very vocal and articulate opposition who were prepared to drag issues and slow down any tempo that Limann had calculated. Behind the scenes, the Military Intelligence, faced with the scare of poised-up junior officers group and a radicalized ranks, had to quickly take measures to stabilise the situation. And Limann would listen to any advice from the Military Intelligence, for external pressures on him, coming mainly from the West, dictated that certain drastic measures would have to be taken if another "leftist coup" was to be avoided. (The Western press had already dubbed the AFRC a leftist regime.)

Rawlings himself had become an enigma. From his vibrant messages backed by boldness and sincerity on 15th May to a challenging and tumultuous June 4, he posed a problem for any leader who did not have much self-confidence and equally powerful charisma.

West Africa magazine, published in London, was quick to react to Rawlings going back into the Forces as a pilot. Its 1st October 1979 issue said in an editorial:

"It is surely intolerable for President Limann to have such a man as Flt. Lt. Rawlings always in the background at his shoulder conspicuously not in the ranks, particularly after he uttered veiled threats about what will be done if a civilian government does not come up to expectations. A final act of patriotism seems to be demanded of the Flight Lieutenant: that he should remove himself further off."

Months later, in another editorial comment, even after Rawlings was an ordinary citizen, the same *West Africa* magazine wrote in its 7th April, 1980 edition:

"Much has been written in West Africa and elsewhere about the damage that June 4 did in some areas. But it also needs to be said again that there is cause for gratitude and respect for Flt. Lt. Rawlings – for stimulating moral outrage over corruption and exploitation, and for preventing a real revolution (the so-called revolution of June 4 should be renamed the near revolution of June 4). He now has the opportunity to do an even greater service to his country."

What service apart from his professional role as a soldier? Some Western countries offered courses to the AFRC men. But Rawlings said no. "I knew they had something at the back of their minds" he told me. "They wanted all of us away so they could indulge in their crimes and call us names."

Dr. Limann was soon caught in a dilemma. In the barracks, Rawlings was still being referred to as "Chairman" by the other ranks – even by some of the officers. "But I gave salute to any Senior Officer", Rawlings said later.

Then, in the civil sector, the fresh experiment with "constitutional order" soon overwhelmed Limann. Every little point was magnified. Once, he made a remark that Ghana had "no natural allies." The leader of the Opposition issued a statement and asked him to withdraw that remark and correct any impressions created.

Meanwhile the masses were getting restless. With the departure of the AFRC, prices were finding their own levels. Limann thought he could use the Vigilante Groups which were springing up in all parts of the country. Even here there were calls on him to legalise the groups. But pressures were on him to stick to the constitutional order.

To strengthen his hand in Parliament, Dr. Limann went into a working arrangement with the **United National Convention** which placed third in the elections. But this was seen in Opposition quarters as an attempt to drift towards "superficially attractive, authoritarian methods of solving problems."

Meanwhile, internal power struggle within the PNP had begun. But a decision had to be taken on J.J. Rawlings who was likely to be watching the confused start of the Third Republic with glee.

Limann had a habit of inviting Rawlings occasionally for discussions.

"Sometimes I gave him a word of advice; at other times he sought my opinion on some proposals they had," said Rawlings.

Towards the end of October, 1979, the Government issued a statement alleging that Rawlings had demanded the destruction of an AFRC warrant which put some soldiers in prison, thereby asking for their release. The same government statement said that a Committee had been appointed to investigate the case. The government action was criticized in Parliament; but on November 12, the Minister of Interior further announced that five soldiers had broken jail and Government was convinced that it was part of a well-laid plan" involving prison officers, armed soldiers and certain unidentified men.

Rawlings told me later: "I couldn't stand this nonsense anymore."

So, he issued a statement which was published in *The Ghanaian Times.* Part of it said:

"I have been very disturbed at what appears to be a campaign to connect me with the recent escape from Usher Fort Prison…I have up till now kept silent because I did not want to be responsible in any way for creating tension that could disrupt the stability of the country. However, the widely publicized statement of the Minister of Interior, Dr. Ekow Daniels, compels me to make a statement, lest my silence be mistaken for guilt…

"More important, however, than my personal innocence, are the clear indications that this is part of a campaign to discredit the government of the Armed Forces Revolutionary Council of which I was Chairman. The enemies of the June 4 Revolution have been leaving no stone unturned in their effort to reverse the gains that were made by the people of this country during my period in office."

One morning, a newspaper headline read:

Limann Told: Coffers Empty

"Not even a pesewa of the AFRC money had been seen." Limann told the Nation after he had been briefed that the country's coffers were empty. But before any more fingers could be pointed at Flt. Lt. Rawlings, the Special Tribunal came out with a statement that all the money collected by the AFRC – running nearly 24 million cedis – were intact, and that more deposits were being made.

One afternoon, President Limann invited Flt. Lt. J. J. Rawlings apparently to discuss if he would accept being made a member of the Council of State, an advisory Council demanded by the Constitution.

Jerry Rawlings had always thought that, given the option, he would go and farm in the Afram Plains.

At the time Limann was making smiles at him in the Castle a radio announcement was saying:

"Flt. Lt. J. J. Rawlings, former Chairman of the AFRC has been retired from the Armed Forces with immediate effect." This was on the advice of the Armed Forces Council on the ground that his continued stay in the military 'was incompatible with his status as a former Head of State."

Five other top officers, including the Army Commander Brigadier Arnold Quainoo and Police Chief C. O. Lamptey, were also retired. So was Chief of Defence Staff, Brigadier Nunoo-Mensah.

The next stage of the trial of J. J. Rawlings had begun!

November 27, 1980 – 65 days after the hand-over.

CHAPTER 7

JUNE 4 "RETIRED"

One of the external props of the PNP regime was the CPP (Overseas Branch) based in London. Its mouthpiece, **THE DAWN**, had given full support to Dr. Limann's PNP because the party purported to be committed to Nkrumaist policies.

But when the London boys began to be disappointed with the performance of the PNP, particularly with the retirement of J. J. Rawlings, the **DAWN** minced no words:

"The PNP blundered in the way it dismissed Flt. Lt. Rawlings...It is understandable that President Limann should fear the popularity of the charismatic Jerry Rawlings. But to dismiss him, and his most prominent colleagues in this cavalier manner, showed weakness, not strength."

In the judgement of the paper, "Jerry Rawlings was the product of deep-seated and justifiable discontent among the lower ranks of the Armed Forces and Police and among the suffering civilian masses. He had no political pretentions, ideological understanding or comprehension of the forces he was unleashing. He was straight forward and sincere to the point of naivety. But the masses instinctively warmed to him".

The **DAWN** was of another view:
"He obviously could not go back flying aeroplanes. But a government that was strong in political acumen and clear about its programme, could have made use of Jerry Rawlings in other ways. If, for example, the Government had launched a National Food Committee, it could have given Rawlings the job as part of the National Food Committee, of organizing the rank and file of the Armed Forces alongside the civilian masses in practical work of economic reconstruction."

As the paper rightly saw:
"Rawlings has shown that he has the ability to incite enthusiasm and dedication. To waste these natural gifts is a terrible mistake."

Incidentally, both the PNP Government and the Opposition were in favour of the dismissal. With June 4 retired, the constitutional way of governing would have full rein.

Meanwhile, all the political parties set up an inter-party consultative committee under the Vice Chairman Dr. J. W. DeGraft Johnson, "to fight trade malpractices and other social evils within the country."

Mr. Victor Owusu, leader of the PFP, called for the immediate dissolution of the Vigilante Groups to avoid "inter-party fights."

He told newsmen that reports from his party members in the regions said some of the Vigilantes "even go to the extent of demanding PNP membership cards before permitting people to buy essential commodities sold under their supervision".

Within the PNP, the Association of Past Students of the Kwame Nkrumah Ideological Institute called on Dr. Limann to abandon his "Welfare State Idea" because "it was advanced stage of capitalism which will not just be suitable for developing Ghana."

From the Opposition, the Parliamentary spokesman Kwaku Baah told a press conference, "After three months of PNP administration – there is a widespread feeling of despondency and insecurity among Ghanaians".

As far as Nana Okutwer Bekoe (Chairman of the PNP) was concerned, the running inflation could be reversed if Ghanaians had a "common front". He was addressing a party rally to explain the budget.

Meanwhile, news leaked from the founder of the PNP, Imoru Egala, that the Ministry of Trade had granted import licence worth ¢10 million to a fishing company, Attok Fisheries, owned by Nana Okutwer Bekoe.

Nana Bekoe rebutted that Egala was not a spokesman for the PNP and so he should shut up.

On another front, a leading member of the opposition PFP, B. A. da Rocha, said in Parliament that Flt. Lt. Rawlings should be called upon to mount an anti-coup campaign in the Armed Forces.

Response from the public was quick, but only published by an independent daily **The People's Evening News**. One reader said that as long as "we accommodate cheating and conceal crime" and as long as "we continue to react only when we are personally affected by injustice…" there will be coups.

On May 12, 1980 the **People's Evening News** carried a front-page story under the banner headline:

STOP THIS ATTACK ON RAWLINGS

On this issue, a traditional leader, Nana Egya Otu Impraim, was saying at a symposium that, instead of the "unwarranted attacks" on members of the erstwhile AFRC, Ghanaians should concentrate on rebuilding the nation.

Nana Impraim noted that, like in the case of Nkrumah, some of those who chanted Hallelujah in praise of Rawlings and his AFRC were the same people saying "crucify them."

While these veiled attacks on the AFRC were going on, a number of students from the Universities had spear-headed the formation of progressive organizations, namely the June 4 Movement, the New Democratic Movement, and the People's Revolutionary League of Ghana.

The New Democratic Movement said in its inaugural statement:

"The hopes which the bulk of our people entertained of a better life (after handover to civil rule) are fast proving to be an empty dream…

"Government positions on crucial national issues have tended to be superficial and partisan while the views of the opposition on such matters have been unprincipled and have tended to centre around pseudo-constitutional issues totally irrelevant to the pressing needs of the masses."

Indeed, on 28th April, 1980, the broad headline in the **Daily Graphic** had read: LIMANN ASKED TO RESIGN.

It was the Third Force Party appealing to Dr. Limann to resign "in order to preserve the constitutional order and save Ghana from total collapse."

Dr. Bilson, the leader, said "the current national mess in which the country finds itself is eloquent confession of failure and admission of the fact that the longer Dr. Limann stayed in office the more disastrous the consequences will be for the nation."

Other concerns of the politicians included:

Ban Farmers Council – PFP
PNP law students want genuine polls!
Disqualified PNP Men Must Quit
PNP Congress Must succeed!
Don't lobby for Posts – Krobo tells Party Men
New Voters List Needed – PFP
Suspend Re-opening of Voters Register
Apaloo is still the Chief Justice – Victor
PNP, UNC Alliance In Danger!

Meanwhile the masses were getting impatient. Food prices had shot up. PNP promises that the Christmas would be "different" had not materialized. The queues were getting longer.

The People's Revolutionary League of Ghana was born at this time. It was inspired by Rawlings' last words in Parliament House:

"We of the AFRC, in light of our reading of the situation, make a fervent appeal never to lose sight of this new consciousness of the Ghanaian people. Never have the eyes of so many been focused on so few. The few are you, the illustrious members of the new administration. The many are those in the factories, in the farms, in the dormitories and junior quarters who will be watching you with eagle eyes to see whether the change they are hoping for will actually materialize in their life time."

This Movement had already been conceived in August 1979 to embrace "all the working people, democratic, progressive and radical sections, from all existing parties, organisations, to protect and promote the interests of the working people of Ghana in particular, and all suffering people in general."

Within the Armed Forces, a purge unprecedented in Ghana's history was going on. The victims were known as activists in the AFRC era. Some were imprisoned and tortured; others simply discharged.

It was getting clear that the PNP and, indeed, its whole constitutional arrangement had not mapped out any clear programme to solve the problems on the ground.

What was Jerry Rawlings going to do now that he was retired, unemployed and still very young?

He told a **BBC** Correspondent:

"*Right now, I find myself compelled to defend the June 4th uprising because I can see, some of us in fact can see, what seems to be an attempt at a castration to give people the impression that what happened on the 4th June was a nightmare to be forgotten, to be thrown overboard – and don't forget, they control the news media, and so long as they go on peddling and pumping out these distortions, their notions of what is right and wrong or what is truth, there is no telling the damaging effect this can have on the people...So I have to keep people on their toes by giving talks here and there.*"

In fact, Jerry Rawlings spent most of his time talking to Chiefs here and there, and appealing to them to release lands for members of the June 4 Movement and other unemployed young people to undertake agricultural ventures. He also accepted lecturing appointments from other supporting Movements born out of June 4.

The first anniversary of June 4 came in 1980. That day, Flt. Lt. Rawlings spoke at a Press Conference, calling on Parliament to seriously investigate what seems to be a campaign of reprisals against certain members of the Armed Forces for their role in the June 4 uprising.

Observing that such reprisals were the very cause of instability in the Armed Forces, Flt. Lt. Rawlings said the campaign also threatens harmony between the Armed Forces and the Civil sector.

He said since the AFRC handed over power to an elected civilian government, there had been a lot of misleading analysis and proposals in respect of the situation within the Armed Forces following the June 4 uprising.

Some of the commentaries, Rawlings said, had gone as far as to attack not only the integrity of the Armed Forces but to question the existence of the Armed Forces in Ghana. The action of the junior ranks on June 4, he said, marked the beginning of an important stage in the history of the Forces. Those who failed to recognize the positive aspect of the June 4 uprising and characterized it simply as an act of indiscipline, were advocating a policy which "could only collide with the wind of change and create an unstable situation in the Armed Forces…"

Flt. Lt. Rawlings said the present system of discipline which was inherited from the past was based on the blind subordination of junior ranks to superior rank – a system known in the Forces as *obey before you complain.* He said this authoritarian military code prevented the corruption of senior officers from being questioned and exposed by juniors. It enabled soldiers to be used in defending on oppressive system which benefitted only a handful of people.

Touching on the gains of the June 4 Revolution, Flt. Lt. Rawlings said it gave birth to a new spirit of awareness among Ghanaians, a mood of insistence on rights by people who had long lived up to their responsibilities without reward or even acknowledgment. The June 4 uprising also gave birth to the realization that power was from the people and that those who rule were not doing Ghanaians a favour for which they could be left at their mercy.

The gains, he observed, had aroused the hostility of the enemies of the people at home and abroad, adding *"those who only gain when the people lose and who lose when the people benefit are desperate to reverse the gains of the people."*

Rawlings said the enemies of the revolution were busy inventing lies, seeking to discredit the revolution and slander its personalities to suit their own purposes. The real aim of this vicious campaign is to demoralize and confuse ordinary people and make them believe that they could not function without a privileged minority of exploiters as June 4 Revolution would have them believe.

Flt. Lt. Rawlings appealed to the youth of Ghana to find courage to reject a "system which had failed us and outworn traditions which deepened our plight."

He said June 4 also showed that even the most powerful persons could be punished for their crime against the people and that *"those very common people, long-suffering as they might be, would one day shake off the chains with which the slave-master sought to hold the captive."*

What words to say only nine months after relinquishing power!

The next day, June 5, a symposium that was to be held at the Accra Community Centre under the auspices of June Four Movement turned out to be a rally. The crowd, milling the spacious centre, could not be contained in the Hall. It was a unanimous decision that the crowd be moved to the park in front of the Community Centre. The speakers, including Flt. Lt. Rawlings, were standing on top of the roof of the Centre. Newspaper estimates of the crowd put the figure at 200,000. Some stood on vehicles while others perched between trees and roof tops nearby.

"The spirit of the June 4 can never be chased out of Ghana," JJ Rawlings said amidst wild cheers. *"The mobilizing force behind it, the dynamic energy of its adherents and historically proved and tested significance of its impact could help every well-meaning and honest government to create a just society in which the welfare of the majority of the people stands supreme.*
Long Live the People!
Long Live the June 4 Movement!
Long Live Ghana!"

After the symposium/rally, the crowd burst into singing a tune in a local language translated as:

"J. J. wake Up!
Limann wants to destroy your people"

The crowd moved into a procession and marched chanting towards the Osu Castle, Office of the President.

The repercussions could well be imagined. There was no doubt that Jerry Rawlings was the people's leader. The massive unplanned demonstrations rocked the foundations of any power which the Constitution had purported to give the PNP government under Dr. Limann.

The reaction of the government was swift. Rawlings had to be eliminated – but with a lot of caution, for fear of invoking the wrath of the masses.

First step was to follow the movement of his close friends – Captain Tsikata (rtd.), Brigadier Quainoo (rtd.) P. V. Obeng, etc. Even when they went to a funeral, these personalities were trailed by the Military Intelligence or Special Branch.

CHAPTER 8

IMPRESSIONS AND SURVIVAL

Sometime in 1980 when I began work on this book, the problem I had was with making appointments with J. J. Rawlings. In his little one bed-room flat on the Independence Avenue, visitors streamed in and out and I wondered whether he was ever going to have time for me. At times, there would be six people all virtually talking to him at the same time about one thing or other.

One morning, after signing the Visitors Book handled by an unenthusiastic policeman posted there by the PNP regime, I entered his hall to find four young men. One was a pressman seeking an interview; another was an unemployed young fellow looking for a job; the third was a soldier who had sneaked in to say hello, and the fourth was a middle-aged woman who had come to inquire about the health of the family.

After helping myself to a cup of coffee, I could not help but listen to the conversation taking place due to limited space in the sitting room. This was not an intrusion as he generally expected others to participate in whatever issue being discussed.

My turn came around 12:30 p.m. He realized we needed time to be alone. So he invited me for a ride in his Peugeot car.

"Surviving has not been easy", he began. "One has to create impressions to be able to survive. You see those men going there?"

He pointed to three smart-looking soldiers crossing into 37 Military Hospital.

"They are comrades but the Intelligence has kept them off me. They know my car; they saw me, but they are scared of someone noticing they are talking to me." He turned towards Burma Camp and kept talking: "I am talking about isolation. Do you understand?"

It was difficult to feel the same way he was feeling but it was easy to see it on his face. It was as if he was saying: "Is that the price for risking my life to create awareness in this society?"

Jerry Rawlings has never minced words castigating those who suppressed his own freedom, as well as that of other people who shared his sentiments.

Occasionally, he seemed worried about how the underdog did not see that he had to play different roles in order to survive. He said:

"For instance, whenever I wanted to be alone, I ended up going to the Continental Hotel.

"I quite clearly saw from the faces of fellow underdogs around the place how dejected and down-spirited they were as they saw me enter the place as if to say 'so are you now identifying with these big men?'

"I felt an urge to explain to them what the situation actually was: If only they could take the trouble to come inside themselves, they would see that I was alone sitting on the balcony because the big men didn't like me either. But, here again, there was nothing one could do because they either had no access to the place or probably they didn't bother to come inside to find out how things actually were."

At one point, I asked why he decided not to live an easy life. As a past Head of State, why did he not live comfortably, moving among V. I.P.s and generally living a good life?

He laughed loudly, slowed down the vehicle and parked near a khebab seller and went out to buy four sticks and offered me two.

We stopped for a while and continued our conversation. He removed his sunshades and began again:

"Yeah, you see. Probably you've heard this thing about my habit of wearing sunshades, being associated with marijuana-smoking and all that. There is a way in which they use it to their advantage, either through their whispering campaign or through these anonymous pamphlets which they pass around or getting some of these stupid private newspapers to create certain impressions. All these are designed to undermine whatever natural authority you enjoy with the people. In effect undermining whatever political presence you have".

I kept listening. He continued: "Sometimes they carry it so far as to distort even your association with men. As I was saying before, they create the impression that one is indulging in subversion when one is clearly not. But the idea is to ISOLATE you. The aim is to cut all my links or connections with the soldiers, with the barracks, or even with the masses. And they do it so successfully that it is imprinted on people's minds".

I interrupted by citing the case of the jail-break which was stage-managed to see Rawlings as the ring leader.

"Ahaa! Yes, they wanted to go on poisoning and misinforming the minds of the soldiers. They made it impossible for soldiers to call on me.

"Quite clearly they knew that if I got access to them, I would prove their stories wrong and word would get back that what the Government was saying was false. And that would destroy the false impression they were creating about me so they had to ensure that counter information – the truth - would not get back so that anybody who contacted me would easily be slotted into the compartment of being an accomplice in subversion. Thereafter, their exercise became successful in misinforming the people".

When Jerry started the car again, I thought I should take over the talking. I gave him my mixed impressions about the AFRC rule, and he burst out into a kind of laughter which is associated with him when he is trying to contain bottled-up feelings.

In the course of interviewing a number of people about how they felt about Jerry after the handover, one military officer gave me his own experience.

"It was at the Osu Cemetery. We were burying a colleague. This was in 1980. Jerry appeared in his casuals and was part of the sympathizers. I clearly noticed some soldiers acknowledging his presence but yet shying off for fear the Intelligence people would blacklist them. It was a kind of an uneasy relationship among close comrades."

There were instances where soldiers and officers who were seen or suspected to have any contact with Jerry were falsely charged, interrogated, imprisoned, sometimes in condemned cells and later dismissed from the Armed Forces. Some still bear the scars of inhuman treatment during their interrogation there.

Such was the life which Rawlings had to live after handing over power to a civilian regime. Interpretations vary, and it is therefore possible that the element of isolation was applied to the maximum against this young soldier whose mere relationship with any man constituted danger to the security of the Nation.

Jerry volunteered information one day in his house on how he had to use relationship with females (since it was difficult relating to any man) as cover for his movements.

"You see, with a woman, it is easy for people to jump to conclusions when she is seen with men. It is easier that way than branding her as an accomplice in subversion…"

I interrupted and put in a question:

"This question of using people – ourselves, and others. Would you say that an example is the way Nkrumah used women to make men wake up when he trained women pilots? I think this was an attempt to break through a barrier of confidence – people think, "This is too complex for us" and then they saw women doing it".

Jerry nodded. "Yes I know it isn't too complimentary to women to have to say "even a woman can do it". But, unfortunately, that is still the dominant attitude. For me it was just a question of using the narrow and parochial interpretations given to man-woman relations as a decoy to outwit the national intelligence apparatus. But then why didn't I employ Nana? She is my wife".

I looked into his face while he continued: "Precisely because of that she didn't fit into some of these roles. It is foolishly assumed that if a man is married a few years, he doesn't devote much leisure time to his wife, but with a girlfriend. However, I remembered some years ago when my wife in her seventh month of pregnancy was used as hostage – she and I knew she could die in the process, but as I keep on saying, there are more painful experiences in life than dying. A man must learn to live and die for a cause".

Jerry paused and lit a cigarette before starting again:

"But then, the MI saw it differently. If I had used my wife for some of those activities the MI would have been suspicious simply because that is how their minds work. They were dumb-stupid, most of them. Some of them were, however, good and supportive – I could see it deep in their eyes. They didn't dare show it – but I could tell."

Jerry could not stop talking about the MI. He was quite incensed about that institution.

"There are some who wanted to pitch their skill and judgement against mine. Some were wise enough to give up, in whatever theatre of activity where they realize their limitations. But there are those who did pay the price for it."

Jerry took a pen and tapped it softly on his table, smiling between the puffs of smoke. He was talking again:

"One night for example, two members of the security who persisted with their usual nonsense on the way from Legon died at the Tetteh Quarshie roundabout when their blue Mazda somersaulted several times…

"I even stopped my car, got down and headed towards their up-turned car with the intention of offering them a lift in mine and telling them to learn the tricks of the game before taking on such assignments…But they were dead."

I was getting more interested in the discussion, so I cut in by returning to the old question:

"It seems that there are some difficult moral issues when it comes to using people. Where is the line between use and misuse?"

Flt. Lt. Rawlings looked at me straight in the eyes, and began, rather slowly:

"You see, generally the line involves consent. That is total commitment implies willingness to be used. But sometimes consent is not possible.

"When I was taking my wife's younger sister to school in Ho, I couldn't tell her my other purpose…"

Jerry paused and then said: "You see, we cannot at this stage expose all our past activities because some of the modus operandi are still being used but…I could give you another example. When a raid was being planned by the security agents to eliminate me, I got wind of their plans and so instead of a location of their choice, I started visiting a friend in town. This forced them to change their theatre of operation to the locality of my choice, where I had placed a counter force, and in the end their plan could not be carried out because the stakes were too high".

The best I could do was just to imagine the scenario. I looked at the clock hanging above Jerry. It was 11:30 p.m. I hadn't thought it was that late. But that didn't rush me anyhow. I was bent on listening further. I responded to an invitation to serve myself another cup of coffee, at the same time listening as he recounted:

"There are citizens of this country (and a few non-Ghanaians) men and women, young and old, some in government positions, serving and retired military personnel and civilians who deserve the highest medal of honour for helping in various was to bring about as well as helping to secure the revolutionary fervor. They are not known and shall never be known. They have chosen to remain anonymous. They may never be decorated. They have chosen to remain anonymous: that is the way it should be and I respect them for it because the battle is not yet over."

This particular bit reminded me of a story one such citizen whom it took me quite a time to convince to talk to me. He told me, "the struggle is a permanent one. I have suffered and continue to suffer under the Limann regime simply because of my total commitment to May15 and June 4, and quite naturally because of my relationship with Flt. Lt. Rawlings".

I shall call him K.P. because he insisted on anonymity. He was not more than 26 years old when I met him in 1981. He had lost his career in the Armed Forces and the government would not countenance his working with any establishment. For almost two years, he moved from job to job living away from his family and heavily intimidated.

"You see", he was saying, "it all started immediately after the handover to the PNP regime, It was as if the Military Intelligence people had been instructed to deal with any June 4 supporter who stood and spoke against cheating, corruption and injustice".

K. P. took a pen and made as if he was jotting down a few notes, but he continued: "As a young soldier imbued with a high sense of patriotism after the June 4 Revolution, I was quite enthusiastic taking part in one of the Limited Infantry Units bush exercises.

This involved map-reading and tactics. It was highly contested for and five infantry units were competing for positions…"

Here, K. P. smiled. I smiled back, and he went on:

"Most of us in the troop knew our Commander was lost but nobody could gather the courage to point it out to him. I decided to help. I went forward and suggested that I try my luck. After a great deal of hesitation and difficulty, he handed over the map and compass to me.

"I decided that we all march back to the starting point. The first miracle came about an hour later. We located an Army jerrycan full of water. That was supposed to be our first objective. Everyone, including the Commander cheered in jubilation…Are you following?"

K. P. definitely saw me rapt in attention. I nodded for him to go ahead.

"Not long after, I led the Unit to locate the second item, which was kenkey hidden in a basket two miles from the first one. From then on, the rest of the items became very obvious to locate.

"And what do you expect? The exercise was so successful that my friends carried me shoulder high and nicknamed me the 'Bush OC', jubilating with the other Units which competed…

"That was where my big problem began. The OC shouted on the troops to stop the jubilation. This didn't work, so he got angry, removed his rank and handed it to me saying that if they wanted me to be the OC, he could make me one. It took some time for the Company Sergeant Major to control the situation".

I sighed heavily and K.P. saw I was following the story. He had more to say:

"When we got back to the Barracks, I was locked in the Guard Room, charged with mutiny…This annoyed most of the boys in the troop, and some of them voluntarily joined me in the Guard Room while others protested vehemently. The Intelligence Officer, sensing danger, called for our immediate release before the Brigade Commander could even arrive…"

"Is that all?" I enquired when he seemed to have got to the end of the story.

"No," he emphasized, continuing:

"Weeks later, promotions came. Because of the last incident it was glaring that only favourites had been considered. There was a clear case of two persons among the ten promoted whose documents had still not arrived at that time.

"The Senior Non-Commissioned Officers (SNCOs) were very much annoyed because those recommended had been by-passed. The SNCOs insisted on justice and fair play, and we were later promoted. Few days later, I was nominated on merit to attend together with another NCO, a course at the School of Infantry. I came back three months later full of enthusiasm for my profession duty consciousness."

I smiled and he replied he hadn't finished. He said:

"Within a short time, my Unit organized a shooting competition in which I took part. When the competition ended, the OC recommended that my rank be reduced from a Lance Corporal to a private soldier. My offence: I had missed one round onto a fallen plate target. Will you believe it...all the ten soldiers who went to the OC to plead on my behalf were dismissed as a warning to the courageous ones who might also dare to plead for me...That was the end of my career in the Armed Forces."

For the next year it was hell. KP narrated how he struggled to get a job in a private timber industry in the Western Region as a clerk. But that lasted for only four weeks. His manager told him there were instructions from above to lay him off.

Few weeks later, K. P. landed another job with Ashanti Goldfields Corporation as Security Officer. "I loved my work," he said. "But alas! The underground Manager called me one morning and showed me a letter from the PNP Government at the Castle asking for my immediate dismissal from the Corporation."

"The Manager, feeling very sympathetic, expressed his preparedness to assist me start a new life. My dismissal letter was handed over to me that evening...."

That was not all for K.P. The next morning, while packing up, the Military Intelligence came in an air-conditioned Range Rover to send him down to Accra. He narrated further:

"In Accra, Dr. Nabila, the Minister of Information and Presidential Affairs, asked if I could come to work with the Castle. I said no, and he warned that I would not get job anywhere if I refused the offer".

K.P. took up the challenge and sought a vacant position at the Cocoa Marketing Board as a Loading Clerk. But true to Dr. Nabila's prediction: "I was paid off after only three weeks", K. P. said. I felt very sympathetic listening to his story. What did K.P. do from then?

"I decided to locate our Chairman, "Flt Lt. Rawlings. When I told him my story, he went very sad and advised that I go to my village up-North to help my old folks. I took his advice. I had no money then, so he borrowed from a friend who was with him and game me some money for transport…"

Just when I was about to interrupt, K.P. cut in again:

"I should have told you this. One morning, just before I was about to leave for the North, Dr. Nabila sent for me again. And this time he warned me that as a Northerner I did not have to follow rogues, and that if I continued, I would die, in his own words, 'like a fowl'".

K.P. said he went back to Chairman Rawlings and told him about it.

"The Chairman took it calmly, shook his head and stood up. He opened his sitting room door slightly and pointed to me two cars parked in front of the house. He said they were from the Military Intelligence, I peeped nearer. Their eyes were red and some of them looked drugged...But the Chairman told me later that he was aware of all their designs and it certainly reminded him of a warning that Fidel Castro's brother gave him in Havana while presenting him with a sub-machine gun. Chairman said he didn't believe it at the time but now he is seeing it in his own eyes, and he thinks it is too late for anything..."

I was about to ask further questions but K.P. was anxious to say a lot more. "You see, Chairman said he could tell me more shocking things being done against his friends but even the little he mentioned made my suffering diminish".

At this point, my pen got short of ink and I asked K.P. to spare me his. I was fully engrossed in the account which was flowing from K.P.

"Chairman told me that it was difficult for certain people to believe it but he was going to tell me a few of the evil designs of the Military Intelligence. He said one day a Catholic Priest-friend of his told him that Capt. Tsikata was in condemned cells; he needed medical care as a result of the heavy beating, so the Prison authorities took him to the hospital. When the Government (of the Acheampong regime) heard this they ordered that he be sent back to the cells.

"Outside his cell, they put a coffin, waiting for him to die. The Catholic Priest said he was there to pray for him, but Capt. Tsikata rather advised him to pray for Ghana...

"Chairman told this so calmly that I nearly dropped tears. He said he knew what the Military Intelligence was capable of doing and that their operations had not changed…He also narrated that one day when Brigadier Arnold Quainoo was at the Military Academy to get a few things typed out for him the Military Intelligence machine-gunned his car. Only God saved him…

"And that is what the M.I. had come to. As long as you are the Chairman's friend or supporter of June 4th you are an enemy of the M.I."

After a few minutes of silence, I asked K.P. how he himself was feeling.

"Honestly, when I heard all this, I began to understand for the first time some of the things Chairman used to say during June 4…This time, he looked like living with death, yet amazingly he didn't look disturbed. Rather I felt a sudden hatred and anger for the M. I. One moment, Chairman, as if reading my thoughts, said I shouldn't hate them because they did not know what they were doing. He told me that they were only pawns in the hands of the manipulators."

KP had more stories to tell:

"On another occasion, I met one soldier who told me about a plot to eliminate Flt. Lt. Rawlings in 1980 on the Aburi hills:

"That time, my unit had gone to Lebanon on United Nations duties and were on stand-by.

"Word came that they were selecting some soldiers to escort Flt. Lt. Rawlings to the Aburi Police Station. I was not selected, the

Military Intelligence knowing that I was a Rawlings supporter; but God so good my very close friend, K. B., was in the team. Early the next morning K. G. came to blow alarm that Chairman was going to be killed. To be frank, tension rose in the barracks, and some of us spread the news in town.

"Luckily, by mid-day another news came that J. J. had been released. Everybody was happy".

Sometime in 1985, after nearly four years of the 31st December Revolution, I talked to Jerry John Rawlings, drawing him back to some of the statements he himself had made, and his experiences and those of others.

I saw it was a chance for him to make what I considered some very deep and fundamental analyses:

"In terms of Revolution, there are two categories of people. There are those whose boundaries are between life and death, to whom survival is necessary in order to act for the benefit of the masses...

"And there are those to whom life is defined by their livelihood, their future, their security, their desire to be comfortable...

"Those who talk as though they belong to the first category, and live as though they belong to the second, are merely riding on the backs of the people's Revolution."

Jerry still felt the need to refer to some of the past experiences:

"Still talking about those days, I was working closely with some of our intellectuals at the University of Ghana in Legon. Since I was being closely watched by the Military Intelligence, I needed a cover to give me the excuse to visit Legon which would seem harmless in their eyes. So, one day, when we had all met together, I asked one of the ladies there if she would pose as my companion; because if the Military Intelligence thought she was my girlfriend, they would think nothing of my going up and down to Legon. She refused because she was afraid. Of what? I don't know – maybe her reputation, fair enough – but..." Jerry was lost in words. He was getting excited now. He said, after a pause:

"I wonder whether she, and some of the others there, know what revolution means despite regarding themselves as revolutionary intellectuals. The ability to conceptualize is valueless without the ability to organize, to act and to sacrifice. Look..." He was on his feet now, taking short steps towards the window overlooking the sea:

"I have personally had to subject myself to humiliating and damaging experiences, but ...." Jerry said and turned towards me, still talking:

"I have no regrets about the use or misuse of myself, if other people couldn't do the worst for fear of pain, death or reputation. A few of us had come to terms with ourselves- for the cause of Ghana, we were prepared to sacrifice our lives, our everything...", and then:

"Those who have declared their commitment to Revolution should be prepared to use themselves. But I have no patience with those who always expect someone else to go and always risk his life and reputation to capture the "beast" whilst they always sit back advising him what to do with it."

Jerry Rawlings was naturally philosophizing. He must have been feeling a deep pain thinking about some of the experiences in his own revolutionary life. I began to feel moved as he reflected quietly:

"We are the living dead. We have already given up our lives. We have laid down for the cause all normal warmth, all placid happiness as obstacles to our commitment, not to ourselves but to a greater end…

"And yet, maybe we are the ones who know a fleeting joy, a bond of love far stronger and deeper for being snatched under the weight of duty…

"We live, we are alive, more than those whose little worlds, filled with unchanging calm or petty incidents, pass fleeting by. They just pass and are gone but we live, our sacrifice intensifies our lives now and even beyond death…"

CHAPTER 9

THE PEOPLE, THE PEOPLE!

I have always been suspicious of political leaders, civilian or military, who play on the term 'The People'. Government by the people, for the people. Food for the Masses. The People's Interest First. We are putting the Commanding Heights of the Economy in the Hands of the People. More Houses for the PEOPLE.

Normally the insincere ones would be filling their bellies as they mouth the slogans.

Ghanaians had heard all these before Jerry Rawlings came on the scene. But when June 4th came, it became clearer that by the people was meant those who had no hand in the production of the basic items the political leaders were talking of. By the people was meant the parasitic few who only complained when their personal interests had been affected.

In any serious public opinion survey, if 60 percent of those interviewed carry a certain opinion, it is taken as public opinion. But the elite in Ghana would always like to paint the pictures that because less than one per cent of the population listen to foreign radio stations it shows public disapproval of the local radio programmes.

If figures are anything to go by, the following research findings should give a picture of how certain notions have been skewed to serve particular interests.

By July 1978, only 50,000 television sets were available in Ghana, reaching an estimated audience of 800,000 (less than one million out of over 10 million people at the time).

Out of the 105,000 copies of the *Daily Graphic* being turned out daily, about half the number was sold in Accra region alone. The *Ghanaian Times* was printing 138,000 copies at the time, and nearly one third of it (46,700) was being distributed in the Accra Region only.

About the same time, rural people constituted 71.1 per cent of the total population; they provided 70.3 per cent of the labour force; produced 98 per cent of food crops and 60 per cent of industrial raw materials for agro-based industries. Rural people also contributed over 96 per cent of the agricultural export produce, earned 60 per cent of the country's foreign exchange and constituted the main source of the county's income generation.

These figures have not changed much over the period, but what is paradoxical is the way the minority elite in the urban areas monopolize almost all the benefits from the sweat of the rural people.

The nine regional capitals which represent only 16 per cent of the population consumed more than 45 per cent of all the goods and services provided by government agencies. When you talk about electricity, the regional capitals consumed over 70 per cent in 1978.

Natural justice demands that those who toil must share the proceeds from their labour. This has been the source of the cry for social justice which J. J. Rawlings began articulating long ago. So that when he repeated several times that sovereignty resides in the people, what he meant was that the majority of the people "should have the power and right to dictate the trend of affairs affecting their lives." This may sound utopian but most developed countries have attained it. "Why not Ghana", Rawlings said, "which is endowed with so much wealth."

Since 1966, Ghana has had varied forms of military intervention. "The Colonels" jumped on the notion that "sovereignty resides in the people" and therefore seized power "in the name of people", their feelings and sentiments quite different from those of the people. And any time a section of the people displayed an action unpleasant to the soldiers, the power of the gun was invoked.

And in the situation where the Armed Forces formed a "professionalized corporation", the senior military officers considered the government as some sort of a client. They could also enjoy in the same way as the professionalized politicians, so why not intervene?

On June 4th, it was not the senior officers taking power with the aid of the junior officers and other ranks. It was the junior officers and other ranks who initiated the action, they themselves feeling like the ordinary and common civilian people of the country. That is why J. J. Rawlings never ceased emphasizing the point that the action of June 4 was motivated by a desire to bring justice – social, economic and political – to all citizens of Ghana. That action, said Rawlings, represented a revolt of the ordinary Ghanaian against social injustices, against economic hardship and against the cancer of corruption that had eaten deep into "the fabric of our society."

Late July 1979, the People's Revolutionary Movement, born out of the June 4 action sent a petition to Flt. Lt. Rawlings asking the AFRC "to take irrevocable steps to ensure that the Revolution is sustained and carried forward to its logical conclusion – beyond October1, 1979 – until all power was vested in the masses and not with the so-called ruling elite." But the AFRC stuck to its programme and pledge.

One of the Movements born out of June 4 and which has survived up till now is the June 4th Movement. This group has identified itself closely with the common people and has earned several derogatory names from the elite. I believe that the impact made by this group has been under-estimated. The Movement originally led by students in the universities, has a large following of workers, teachers, farmers, revolutionary cadres and the unemployed.

The Press Conference beginning the week of celebrations of the Third Anniversary of the June 4th uprising was a historic one. Historic because most of the predictions which had been made on their platform at the two previous anniversaries had come true. This was June 4,1982.

This was a crowded affair. It was difficult to distinguish between a pressman and a cadre.

The political gains of the three months of the Armed Forces Revolutionary Council gave inspiration to the birth of the June 4 Movement.

The Movement carried on the political struggle with the aim of, firstly, preventing the attempts by the privileged upper-class to isolate Flt. Lt. J. J. Rawlings from the masses and thereby physically eliminate him.

Secondly, it was projected that the struggle would subsequently result in the overthrow of the oppressive upper-class rule "to create the necessary favourable conditions for a re-arrangement of the economic system to the benefit of the working people."

The Press Statement read at the Conference alluded to the several attempts by the PNP regime to eliminate Flt. Lt. Rawlings and Capt. Kojo Tsikata (rtd). "Soldiers who were identified with us were arrested and tortured and finally kicked out of the Army. The back-firing of the exhaust pipe of a car was reported as a coup attempt by persons associated with our movement."

The sentiments of members of the June 4 Movement were not different from those of other progressive organizations who believed that the Revolution must continue and that the 31st December Revolution was only the beginning of the end.

J. J. Rawlings had no illusions about who the masses were and how they felt. He had no money to give them, he told large crowds, but "I am here to help you realise that you have dignity! You must insist on your right."

Rawlings has refused to talk ideology in the conventional sense of the word. But he has not been unaware that neo-colonialism has created a political economy in which the ruling elite held both political and economic power – enabling them to hold the masses to ransom. Yet he believed that a long-term programme to wrestle economic power from foreign domination needed time – education, conscientization, mobilization, production, determination and above all confidence of the people.

Even for the soldiers who had been used to hunt their fellow men, there was need for a great deal of education, and this J. J. Rawlings continually undertook throughout the AFRC rule and even into the 31st December Revolution.

There came a time when the PNP Government decided that voters had to be re-registered. The response from the ordinary people was poor, partly because the consciousness of the masses was rising above merely being invited to vote in an election. The Government that had been voted into office was making no visible progress in revamping the economy, let alone give hope to the ordinary people that there was a better future. Reports from Parliament indicated that most days, a quorum was difficult to come by. As a result, the seriousness with which people thought their affairs were going to be deliberated was completely absent. Rawlings noted these points in his 2nd anniversary speech on June 4 1981.

"Given the conditions that the productive majority face these days – the high cost of living, the state of the roads and railways, the conditions in the hospitals – and the high hope that had accompanied the promulgation of the new Constitution and the handover, it is disheartening to observe how the elected representatives of the people are responding to the plight to the ordinary man."

Jerry understood the language of the people, and he articulated it with all conviction and empathy:

"Many people are beginning to feel that political parties only profess an interest in the people when it is voting time only to abandon them in between the elections.

"Meanwhile the rich patrons of these parties are desperate to reap the harvest of what they invested in winning power and constantly use their position for profitable deals. It is no wonder that people seem disinterested in the current voters registration exercise."

The fact that Rawlings was not spewing "ideology" did not mean that he did not understand the social forces operating at the time. Rather, he chose to analyze situations in simple language which the ordinary people could understand. He called on workers, soldiers, farmers, policemen, teachers and students to realize that they cannot expect to have their needs attended to simply because there is a Constitution, or simply because civilians are ruling and not soldiers. He reminded them all that in the history of Ghana "we have seen the capacity of civilians too to flout the Constitution and deny the most elementary rights of the people." His prescription was:

"So ordinary people must constantly struggle to ensure that the ideals enshrined in the Constitution are applied to their situation." But be warned:

"Success in that struggle will require the initiative of workers themselves to organize effectively the forces of progress, to create a common platform with the students, farmers, progressive intellectuals and other patriots and to ensure that victory is not wrenched from their hands…..

"For myself, I am ready for whatever sacrifices are required in such a struggle for a better life for our people, and I will forever work with and be at the service of, the people who share that common cause."

Rawlings did not receive adequate publicity for this press conference but the message went down to the people through the security agencies, progressive forces and politicians who were present at the Community Centre.

At the time, the prospect of real democracy in which the people were masters of their own destiny had dawned on him. He said he knew that there were people in the society who resented the initiatives of working people and who are even frightened at the prospects of real democracy.

"And they expect to obtain peace and security without creating the needed social and economic relationships of justice in the production and distribution of this country's wealth", he told the audience present.

Even before the 31ˢᵗ December Revolution, during which Defence Committees were established as organs of popular power, J. J. Rawlings had no doubt in his mind about grassroots democracy. "The possibility was demonstrated during the June 4ᵗʰ era by the Committees that emerged from within various working groups. I may mention particularly the short-lived Junior Ranks Revolutionary Committee of the Police Service, as well as the way in which soldiers also began to organize committees in their own units."

One of the criticisms against Jerry Rawlings during the PNP regime was that he exaggerated the "gains of June 4". Politicians said openly that they were fed up with "the so-called gains". But one wonders how seriously they took the press conference marking the second anniversary of June 4ᵗʰ.

Rawlings provided enough clues to show that a good number of ordinary people were knocking on his door.

"I have no doubt that we made mistakes and that there were many unfinished tasks."

What were these unfinished tasks?

Rawlings himself gave a hint:

"Ghana today is in the grip of a grave crisis. But the solutions cannot lie in a loss of confidence in our own people and an abject submission to the economic domination of foreigners." That way, he said, Ghanaians would be denying their very sovereignty and would be repudiating the hopes of the forebearers 'who struggle to free us from the colonial yoke.'"

No greater words could have admonished the Limann regime, particularly when he said:

"Those who have their ears turned towards the people will also know what value the people place on the June 4th days as an opening towards their realization of the ideals of Freedom and Justice, our national motto."

And then for those businessmen-turned politicians who were busy amassing wealth, "May we point out to the enemies of the people a very vital lesson of June 4th that clearly has not registered in their minds: that it was the monkey's refusal to pick one nut at a time out of the gourd that led to his downfall."

Any observer at this press conference would easily deduce that Rawlings was a fighter. He was daring and persuasive and the secret of his fearlessness was derived from his conviction that he had authority from the masses of the people.

When he spoke those words, it became obvious that he was prepared to lead the people to regain their freedom. All the efforts of June 4th were being trampled upon under the feet of a constitutional order; and the statelessness of the majority of the people could no longer be described in abstract terms:

"We end by recalling the words of John F Kennedy, many years ago:

"'Those who make a peaceful revolution impossible, make a violent revolution inevitable.'

"Long Live June 4th!

"Long Live Ghana!!"

A standing ovation greeted Rawlings. The masses flocked to him, each one trying to shake his hands. He raised his right fist and the pandemonium was uncontrollable.

It was the beginning of the sounding of the death knell of the PNP regime.

It also provided the security agencies the grand opportunity to intensify their harassment and close surveillance of the movements and activities of Jerry Rawlings and his close associates.

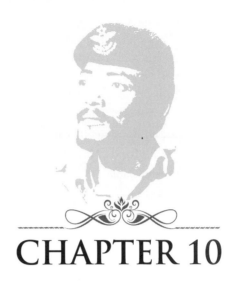

CHAPTER 10

RAWLINGS AND THE 31ST DECEMBER REVOLUTION

If launching of the 31st December Revolution caught popular support, it certainly was not accidental. Not only had June 4th cadres penetrated the work places, villages and the police and military barracks, the spineless of the Limann regime coupled with ineffective opposition alternatives provided the appropriate conditions for a popular revolution.

"We knew it was going to come but we didn't know exactly when", said a member of the June 4th Movement whose task was to do some education work in the Brong Ahafo Region. "Sometimes I would sleep in a village classroom for the week-end just to avoid the hungry security people. We held our meetings in classroom", he told me.

"In fact, a great deal of support also came from the radical PNP Youth Wing some of who spurred us on in our education drive when they saw that power struggle in both the ruling party and the opposition parties had taken precedence over the welfare of the masses", wrote a cadre to me from the Accra Region.

When I asked a soldier from the Air Force to put on paper his own experience, he wrote that the original date for the launching to the Revolution was to be 24th December, 1981, but a day before, some airmen were arrested by the Military Intelligence, "so the action was delayed – but most of us who belonged to the 'Club' were sure that as long as our man was leading us we would move again."

News flashed very fast among the other ranks in the Armed Forces.

"As soon as everybody heard there was going to be a revolution they promised their support, but we had to be careful because the Military Intelligence had bought some of the soldiers."

So F. K. was "always vigilant". His aim towards 31st December was to secure some weapons and keep them somewhere before the operation started. He managed to keep that of his duty-mate, and hid it in a Pinz-gauer which was parked in front of the guardroom. For the few minutes that he went to the hangar, somebody took the weapon and also hid it somewhere. For his punishment for "leaving" his weapon behind, F. K. was locked up in a guard room to be released a few hours later after he lied to his Warrant Officer. He narrated:

"On the 30th of December four Sergeants and three Corporals, plus myself, met in Sgt B.'s house and held our last meeting. We finalized how we were going to attack the Air Force Station...

"When the first gun-shot was heard, I quickly rushed to the Air Force Station and joined my colleagues. All those I met there were friendly forces...We took positions at the hangar to guard the aircraft while a few others stood at the main gate...

"Late in the morning, when my brother J. J. went on radio to announce the beginning of the Revolution, we knew the masses would support it."

Any temptation to under-estimate the popular base of the Revolution would be unfortunate. Occasionally a charge would be made by enemies that the Revolution was "tribal inspired". An appropriate answer, I think, was given by Mr. Johnny Hansen, a veteran politician of the Nkrumah vein, and first PNDC Secretary for Internal Affairs. He spoke to Ebenezer Babatope, a Nigerian writer:

"The charge of tribalism is arrant nonsense...It is a revolution which all the oppressed and over-exploited people of Ghana understand. The basis of our people's support for the Revolution is borne out of our experiences of exploitation".

Of course, most revolutionaries I spoke to or agreed to write their experiences for me, had varying ethnic backgrounds. The common language they spoke was revolution – the need to knock down the old structures which had permitted perpetual exploitation of the masses by a minority few.

This Corporal B. F. who was with the Fifth Battalion of Infantry, sent me this note which I like to produce unedited:

"In my Unit, before the 31st December Revolution, anybody who hears that Jerry is going to lead us then happiness come. After meeting Jerry at Legon I also started sending messages from him to our friends in both Arakan and Gondar barracks, as well as carrying messages from the friends to him. We were 100 per cent sure that we are going to succeed with the support of the masses. On the 11th November, 1981, I was in my house when four men from MI came for me. At the Annex, I was questioned and had some slaps before they released me, but all the same we didn't give up until 30th December 1981 when I was arrested again and this time sent to Sunyani Guard Room (in the Brong Ahafo Region – 300 miles away). I was in the guard room when I hear 3 BN (Sunyani) calling all the soldiers to fall in, and I was just praying the Almighty God to get us through. At about 11 a.m. I heard the voice of Brother Jerry on the air before Maj.-Gen. Quainoo also came; then I became normal being.

"On 1st January, 1982, I escaped from the guard room to join my people in Accra at the Gondar Barracks...The jubilation of the civilians from Sunyani to Accra convinced me that the popular Revolution had succeeded".

On June 5th, 1980, a day after the historic rally involving over 200,000 people in Accra, 6,000 workers of the Ghana Industrial Holding Corporation (GIHOC), the largest single industrial establishment, went on strike to demand for better conditions of service. The workers simultaneously closed down their factories spread across the country – from the North to the South, from the

West to the East – and even locked up some of their Management staff. In Accra, the over 3,000 workers from the Tema and Accra factories charged on Parliament House, disrupted proceedings of the Parliamentarians and said through placards that the elected representatives should be more serious and deal with problems affecting workers.

Some of the workers rushed to the canteen of the Parliamentarians and did justice to the breakfast that was ready.

The response later in the evening was predictable: GIHOC was instructed to dismiss all the workers who went on strike.

On this particular issue, the Constitutional procedures were set aside, and even members of the Opposition agreed unanimously with the government order.

The consent of the Opposition was understandable. Intelligence reports had indicated that the strike must have been masterminded by J.J. Rawlings and his June 4th men who wanted to undermine the stability of the Nation.

For over a year, majority of the workers whose case was being argued in Court were left at the sidelines. Some of those who later lost their jobs when the Government asked them to re-apply had only one option left; to bide their time.

31st December, therefore, was like a festival day for the suffering people, the unemployed and the exploited. They jumped into the streets without prompting and some joined in the looting of shops belonging to particularly the Lebanese and Syrians.

"I am asking for nothing less than a revolution – a revolution that would transform the socio-economic structures of the country".

That was J. J. Rawlings on 31st December, 1981 who further said that he was *prepared to face the firing squad* if what he had initiated was not acceptable to the majority of the people.

It was like wildfire. Soldiers ran into town. Civilians rejoiced and danced. University students in town organized themselves and led demonstrations on the streets of Accra.

The whole world was taken by storm. Foreign newspaper reports deplored the inability of Ghanaians to practice Western democracy. Another constitutional experiment had failed and the Nation had been ushered into a revolutionary era.

Soon after 31st December, one of the workers of GIHOC, Mr. Amartey Kwei, was to be appointed a member of the PNDC.

I had a rare chance to talk to Corporal A. B. who participated actively in 15th May, 4th June and 31st December actions. He had been haunted by the MI after the handover on 24th September, 1979. "One day, I had to run into the bush and then to a friend's house when I got a hint that they were rounding up all the 4th June activists," he narrated. The army later discharged him.

"Some of our boys were locked up at Nsawam Medium Security Prisons for 10 months without trial; one of us crossed the border into Nigeria; another went up North and probably ended up in Burkina Faso...But I had stayed around civilian quarters periodically passing on information and public reaction to Chairman".

A.B. told me that though he has been quite active up till now, there has not been one moment he thought he was giving up.

"A revolution is a revolution; you either believe in it or not. If our leader is still committed to it, how can we give up?" he said.

A.B., unassuming and quiet, told me one day:

"Out of the nine men who struck on 31st December, not one of us is on the PNDC. We prefer staying in the background and still playing an effective role. It is not for positions that some of us joined our Chairman. It was for the sake of mother Ghana."

A.B. explained that because of the homework already done on the ground, and the popularity of the Leader, coupled with the mess created by the PNP regime, several other soldiers joined "in this history-making process to correct injustices in the country."

POSTSCRIPT

MEMORABLE THOUGHTS OF J. J. RAWLINGS

The Press

"The Press is a public press, part of the mechanism of state power, and it is funded by the tax payer, which in Ghana, means the poor masses. In the past, the press had been used against these very people. We now want to be sure that the press will constitute an expression of the people's freedom and not their oppression."

(January 18, 1982)

Education

"It is necessary that we transform an educational system which has bred negative attitude in our students and in the society, generally. This is vital if the Revolution is to strengthen itself and render the public institutions more accountable to those they are supposed to serve."

(April 15, 1982)

"The battle for the mind must be won in this Revolution if we are to make any progress."

(April 15, 1982)

"June 4 and December 31 constitute important landmarks in the liberation of our minds in our psychological preparedness to fight our exploiters and oppressors."

(May 1, 1982)

Revolution

"We have committed ourselves to a revolutionary transformation of our society. That we shall never go back on; but we must remind both critics and admirers that a revolution is not a one-act play which happens once and it's all over."

(May 1, 1982)

"A revolution is a historical process and at each historical juncture we have to act in conformity with the given objective conditions of the time."

(July 29, 1982)

"To work for the Revolution is not only to hit the headlines in the news media but to dedicate oneself continuously to the improvement of the material condition of our working men and women."

(July 29, 1982)

"Our detractors will not succeed in turning us back. Let them know there is no "U" turn. We know it will not easy but with courage, will, determination and your support we shall win.
"Others have done it; we can also do."

(July 29, 1982)

"The 31st December Revolution in Ghana is the culmination of the struggle our people against injustice, indignity and exploitation."

(October 23, 1982)

"The Revolution has come to structure the fundamental basis and institutions of our society to make the people the daily and active participants in decision-making."

(October 23, 1982)

"The 31st December Revolution was initiated on the basis of the confidence in the people of this country, confidence and optimism in the people's ability and determination to bear any difficulty, sacrifice or damages, to create a just, democratic social order in place of the long years of oppression, human degradation and exploitation they have known."

(November 6, 1982)

"A revolutionary process like a heavy rain, you cannot have it without thunder and lightening."

(November 6, 1982)

December 31st was the first act in a
…long process of revolutionary transformation of the socio-economic structure of our country."

(November 6, 1982)

"We have made some mistakes and as revolutionaries we are not reluctant to admit our mistakes openly, and correct them with the aid of analysis and self-criticism."

(November 6, 1982)

GALLERY

The Castle Documents

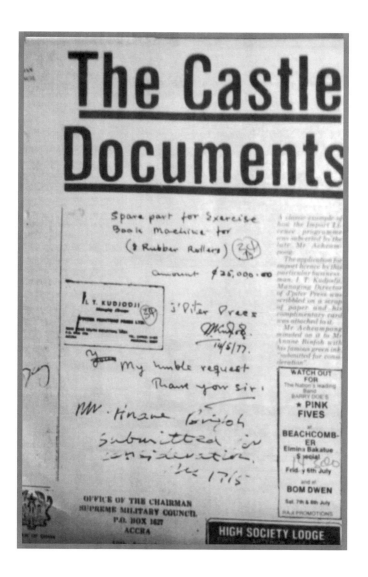

Spare part for Exercise
Book Machine for
(1 Rubber Rollers)

Amount ₵25,000.00

I. T. KUDJODJI

3'Diter Press

14/5/77.

My humble request
Thank you sir.

MR. Kwame Binfoh
submitted in
consideration.
17/5

OFFICE OF THE CHAIRMAN
SUPREME MILITARY COUNCIL
P.O. BOX 1627
ACCRA

AIR VICE-MARSHAL GEORGE YAW BOAKYE

MAJ.-GEN. EDWARD KWAKU UTUKA

REAR ADMIRAL JOY KOBLA AMEDUME

Assets of some Military Officers

A LINE UP OF THE PRESIDENT AND MEMBERS OF THE MILITARY TRIBUNAL WHICH TRIED COUP PLOTTERS OF THE ABORTIVE 15TH MAY UPRISING IN 1979. THE TRIBUNAL WAS CHAIRED BY COL. J.E. ENINFUL

The seven accused persons on trial

Graphic front page headline, May 30th 1979

AFRC Members address the media

AFRC Members address the media

161

AFRC MEMBERS

Flt. Lt. J. J. Rawlings – Chairman

Capt. Boakye Djan – Member

Lt. Cdr. H.C. Apaloo – Member

Lt . K. Baah Achamfour – Member

Maj. Mensah Gbedemah – Member

Maj. Y.A. Mensah Opoku – Member

Pte. Owusu Adu – Member

L.Cpl. Sarkodie Addo – Member

L.Cpl Peter Tasiri Abongo – Member

L.Cpl J. Newton Gatsiko – Member

L.Cpl Fred Ansah Atiemo – Member

Cpl. Sheikh Tetteh – Member

Cpl. Owusu-Boateng – Member

W.o.ii H.k.obeng – Member

S.Sgt. Alexander Adjei – Member

163

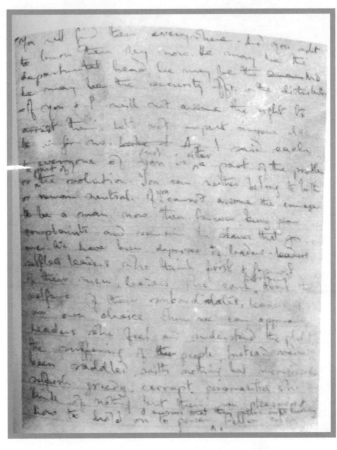

Rawlings' Handwritten Statement At The Time Of Arrest

JJ Rawlings addressing Junior Officers

JJ Rawlings going to inspect a parade at the Sports Stadium

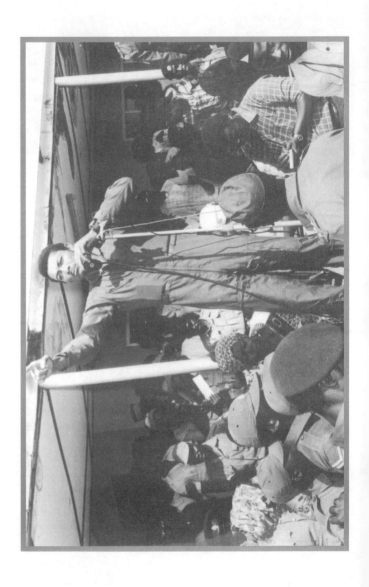

JJ Rawlings addressing students of University of Cape Coast

Students Back Secret Trials

From Noi Lartey,
Kumasi

STUDENTS of the University of Science and Technology yesterday paraded through the principal streets of Kumasi to demonstrate their support for the 'secret trials' and executions by firing squad of eight top officers of the Ghana Armed Forces.

They chanted revolutionary songs such as "let the blood flow" and carried branches of trees and placards some of which read: "Farming not a punishment — kill them all", "Down with foreign pressures", "lawyers do not pay taxes — away with them", "Nigeria hoard your oil — we shall clean our house", "Let the blood flow", "A half revolution is no revolution".

Other placards read: "Elizabeth Ohene, Acting Editor must go," "Can Col. Slater weed? Kill him", "Bar Association to hell with you", and "For heaven's sake, kill".

The students ended their parade at the Ghana National Cultural Centre where the president of the Students Representative Council, Mr Ben Odame, handed a resolution to the Commander of the Fourth Battalion of Infantry, Capt. J. K. Attipoe, to be forwarded to the Armed Forces Revolutionary Council.

The eight-point resolution which was read before it was handed over, condemned in no uncertain terms the unwarranted interference in the internal affairs of Ghana by countries and bodies who had never shown any concern for the suffering people of this country and "who can have no appreciation of the revolutionary process which is unfolding in the country today".

It also called on the AFRC to take firm and revolutionary action against "all the local reactionary forces" like the Ghana Bar Association, the Christian Council, the Catholic Secretariat the so-called non-

• *Contd. on Ps.8/9.*

THERE'S dignity in labour, a bare-chested Flt-Lt. Rawlings demonstrates as he shovels sand, setting a new trend in the hitherto purely ceremonial sod-cutting occasions we used to know.

JJ Rawlings doing "Walatu walasa"

J. J. GOES FISHING

FLT-LT Jerry John Rawlings, Chairman of the PNDC at the week-end went on a fishing expedition with the crew of "FLI-KOHAYO" boat at Tema.

The Chairman undertook the expedition to acquaint himself with the problems facing fishermen.

During the expedition which lasted three-and-a-half hours, Flt-Lt Rawlings ate, smoked and exchanged ideas with the fishermen.

The Chairman arrived at the fishing harbour at about 8 a.m. unannounced but immediately the people noticed the armoured cars a large cheering crowd gathered at the harbour.

He jumped down from the armoured car and went straight to where the fishing boats were moored and asked the fishermen which of the boats was ready to sail.

It turned out to be "FLI-

(Contd. on Pg 4/5)

PDCS

J.J. Rawlings, (middle) sharing with the crew members their breakfast

170

JJ Rawlings helping to load cement on a truck

JJ Rawlings with construction workers

JJ Rawlings addressing Junior Officers at the Region

Workers and students came to the Independence Square to assure support for the Leader of the Revolution.

JJ Rawlings addressing young people

JJ Rawlings addressing political party leaders

Tete-a-tete with Fidel Castro
at the Non-aligned Conference in Havana, September, 1979

JJ Rawlings welcomes Thomas Sankara of Burkina Faso

Courtesy call by President Jimmy Carter of the United Sates of America

JJ Rawlings meets Chiefs

The Constitution calls for the separation of powers of the Presidency and the Parliament.

The Constitution makers realised that when you have President and Parliament from the same party you have the recipe for legalized dictatorship.

The Constitution makers gave Ghanaians a chance to prevent this by insisting on a second ballot.

This is your chance to PROTECT THE SPIRIT OF THE CONSTITUTION.

Together with the P.F.P. your votes in the recent Presidential elections totalled more than ONE MILLION ONE HUNDRED THOUSAND against only some 600,000 for the P.N.P.

We appeal to you how to use your votes to ensure a democratic way of life, for this country. This is no longer a question of personalities it is a straight two way fight.

If you vote for Victor Owusu then the separation of powers, essential to preserve freedom is guaranteed; if you do not vote or vote the other way you will have put executive power and legislative power into the hands of one group of people who have shown us before what they can do with absolute power.

"Power corrupts and absolute power corrupts absolutely". Please do not allow any group to enjoy absolute power.

VICTOR OWUSU

TOLON NA

VOTE MASSIVELY FOR VICTOR OWUSU

PNP

WE ARE ON THE MOVE

The June 18 elections have established our majority in parliament. And to ensure that Ghana succeeds in the Third Republic all that remains to be done is for you to vote for Dr Hilla Limann the P.N.P. Presidential candidate in the forthcoming second round of the elections.

Dr Limann is young, humble and dynamic. Dr Limann speaks fluent French which is a great asset in these days of personal diplomacy as Ghana shares borders with French-speaking countries.

As a historian, economist and political scientist Dr Limann is equipped with the requisite knowledge to cope with the problems facing the country.

By virtue of his training, Dr Limann believes in Government by consensus and is a strong advocate of a vigorous and constructive opposition. Dr Li-

mann will uphold the Constitution and cherish the Rule of Law.

With his humble background as the son of a labourer, Dr Limann has sympathies for the common people as he belongs to a People's Party which is truly national as manifested by the election results since P.N.P. won parliamentary seats in every region.

Remember to vote for Dr Limann on election day; for with the majority in parliament it is only a P.N.P. Government that will guarantee a smooth administration in the country.

Hilla Limann
Presidential Candidate

EYE ABE ARA NA OREKO

J J Rawlings at the Electoral Commission

JJ Rawlings ready to hand over

Limann takes over from Rawlings,
"Never lose sight of the new consciousness." (J.J.R.)

"I intend to remain in the Forces in the same bumble position as I was before,"
Jerry says as he rejoins his Unit after the handover ceremony

Route march through the streets of Accra

JJ Rawlings with Prof Kwesi Botchwey and Mr. Kofi Totobi-Quakyi at the Accra Sports Stadium

Government officials ready for a sporting activity

A panting sportsman JJR speaks to the Press

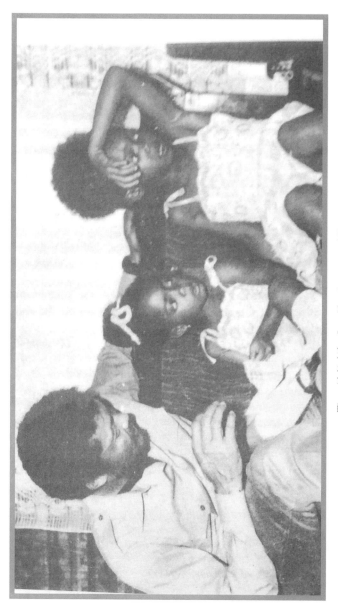

Time with his kids – Jerry, Yaa Asantewaa and Ezanetor

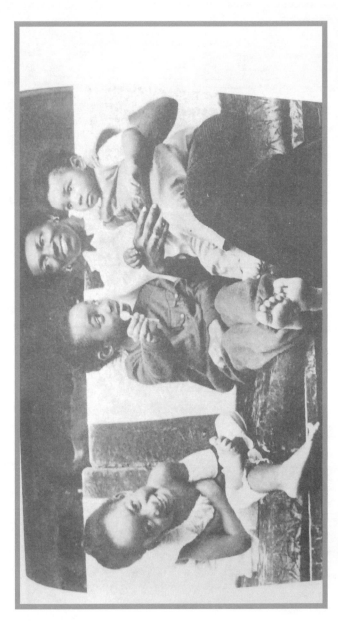

The family behind JJ Rawlings – Ezanetor, 7; Yaa Asantewaa, 5; Amina, 1; and their mother, Nana Konadu Agyeman Rawlings

JJ Rawlings relaxing on the Volta River